A YEAR IN PRAYER

John Torrance

A YEAR IN PRAYER

John Torrance

Yorkminster Park Baptist Church and the
Baptist Convention of Ontario and Quebec

THE BAPTIST CONVENTION OF ONTARIO AND QUEBEC
100 - 304 The East Mall, Etobicoke, ON M9B 6E2

A Y E A R I N P R A Y E R
Written by John Torrance

Printed in the United States.

Editor: Rosemary Aubert
Front Cover Art: Douglas Brown
Interior Illustrations: Sue Ericsson
Author Photograph: West Photo
Design: Dianne Eastman
Text has been set in Berling.

Library and Archives Canada Cataloguing in Publication
Torrance, John, 1943-
  A year in prayer / John Torrance
ISBN 978-0-921028-50-5
    1. Baptists--Prayers and devotions. 2. Church year--Prayers
and devotions. 3. Pastoral prayers. I. Baptist Convention of
Ontario and Quebec II. Yorkminster Park Baptist Church
(Toronto, Ont.) III. Title.

BX6337.T67 2008   264'.06013   C2008-907628-1

Dedicated to Margaret Torrance

who helped make this book possible, and to the

congregation of Yorkminster Park Baptist Church, Toronto,

on whose behalf the prayers were offered.

Thanks be to God.

FOREWORD

Voicing a public prayer in the context of leading worship is a special act. It requires some understanding of the congregation and its context. There is an underlying theological framework that informs the prayer. The leader must have a personal faith for the prayer to have authenticity. Articulate and meaningful words lift hearts and minds as the prayer is spoken.

John Torrance artfully captures all of the best qualities of prayer in this collection of his public prayers. This volume is offered with the expectation that these prayers will live on in the experience of you, the reader, as you reflect on them and offer the prayers again on your own behalf.

Meaningful prayers like these are the result of more than the artful use of words. They come from the depths of a life well lived. John Torrance understands servant leadership and cares deeply for people as part of his commitment to serve God. He has led a number of congregations and is appreciated for his excellent and fruitful leadership. He has served in our Baptist Convention of Ontario and Quebec family of churches on a number of committees and boards, highlighted by a distinguished term as President of Convention. I had the privilege of working alongside him for several years. His integrity and effectiveness were evident. John leads with calm confidence and with a respect for each person.

It is out of the richness of his faith and life experience that John is able to so effectively focus prayers that resonate in the hearts of all who hear or read them. Our gratitude to you, John, for this gift of prayer.

Open your own heart and mind to let these prayers take root in your soul and strengthen your faith.

In Christian service,

Ken Bellous

Executive Minister

Baptist Convention of Ontario and Quebec

PREFACE

Long ago, those close to Jesus asked him to teach them to pray. He didn't give them a manual, but a prayer which was short, yet so profound that it has changed us all. In many ways the traditional Pastoral Prayer is an extension of the Lord's Prayer. In it God's servant seeks to lift before God the matters on the hearts of God's people – matters that need to be confessed collectively in humility: "Forgive us our trespasses as we forgive those who trespass against us," and matters that need to be proclaimed in wonder and praise: "Hallowed be Thy name." As well, the Pastoral Prayer reflects the daily tension between trust and anxiety: "Give us this day our daily bread," and the deep longing for wars, famines, feuds and illnesses to end: "Thy will to be done on earth as it is in heaven."

Like the Lord's Prayer, the Pastoral Prayer is not only an instrument of worship, but also of education. The pastor offers it to God, but does so on behalf of the people, and as they listen they will often find themselves saying 'amen' in deep and often unfamiliar places. It empowers those whose longings are beyond mere words to shape a vocabulary of faith as they discover that they are not alone in their fears and troubles. In this sense it is not only educational, but above all, profoundly pastoral.

The Pastoral Prayer may not be nearly as magnificent as the offerings found in prayer books and other liturgical resources, but it has been born of a pastor's love for the community of faith and when offered in love the prayer is often answered in the hearts of the people long before the choir echoes the amen of everyone's heart.

The Pastoral Prayer is no less heartfelt than the extemporaneous prayers more commonly offered in churches today. In fact, it is probably more heartfelt because it comes from hours of toiling with words and ideas and feelings and issues. During those early morning quiet times when such a prayer often takes shape, the pastor is wrestling with none other than God himself and, therefore, not able to hide behind old familiar phrases. In this sense it is very much a gift born of God's love.

Sunday by Sunday I have been blessed by the prayers offered by my colleague, the Rev. John Torrance. His prayers are not only the result of early morning sessions with God, but also of afternoons spent in hospitals and nursing homes and evenings with the homeless. They have also been shaped by the ministry years he spent building new churches, leading mission teams, presiding over denominational meetings, sitting at a farmer's table, preaching in the national capital, and walking the streets in the heart of a vast city. And above all, they come from the heart of one who is a devoted husband, father and friend, yet still a child.

I commend to you these prayers offered by a faithful servant of God and a dear friend, John Torrance. Unbeknownst to John, this collection of prayers has been assembled and published by the people of the church as a way to mark and celebrate the ministry he has had at Yorkminster Park Baptist Church, Toronto. John has entered into the dance of our days and laughed and sung and walked and wept with us all through the night and all through the day. John is soon to retire, but his prayers shall not fall silent, and they shall be answered as surely as they have already been.

In Christ,

Peter Holmes

November, 2008

INTRODUCTION

On most Sundays for the better part of a decade, members of Yorkminster Park Baptist Church had the great privilege of being led in prayer by John Torrance.

These were traditional "Pastoral Prayers," prayers of guidance for the congregation of a large metropolitan church faced with urban problems at the beginning of a troubling century.

But when I was asked to consider a selection of the prayers for publication, I soon saw that they are, as well, prayers that anyone would be inspired to use for personal devotion.

This led me to the principal rationale for the selection and arrangement of the more than fifty prayers in this book. They can be used, one per week, by a minister with a congregation, but they can also be used for individual prayer by anyone.

The selection follows the natural year, beginning with spring, because John's sense of prayer shows a deep affection for God's physical Creation manifest in the beauty of the seasons.

The prayers collected here reflect a profound faith rooted in the love of Christ, in the work of his Church and in the fellowship of his People.

It was an honour to collect these prayers. In addition to the sense of devotion they arouse, they are also beautifully written and show literary skill of an exceptional quality.

They also reflect the personality of the man who wrote them and the Man who inspired them, the combination of warmth and reality that is at the center of Christian faith.

Rosemary Aubert

CONTENTS

SPRING

Almighty and merciful God, it is in humility that we come to you in prayer, expressing gratitude for the privilege of meeting in worship as members of your family, the church. From you we receive all things that make life sustainable and pleasurable and meaningful; you nourish us in body, mind and spirit; you offer us love and mercy and forgiveness. We confess to you now our need for that forgiveness. We have broken your moral commands, rebelled against your rules for living, hurt others through our temper and selfishness and neglect, and damaged the environment through our polluting ways. May the body of sin that is within us be destroyed, even as we claim forgiveness through the blood of Christ, the One who died for us, that we might "walk in newness of life (Romans 6:4)" in your presence forever.

We pray for a sense of renewal in the lives of others, O God; for those afflicted with injury from accident, and those fighting disease and illness, and those who have been traumatized by murder and crime, and those who need relief from all the stress in their lives. We pray for the healing power of your Spirit to be with the sick. We thank you that we can know peace, in spite of the turmoil about us, because of the assurance that you are always beside us and within us and ahead of us as the Lord of our lives.

We pray for those working to improve the lives of others, to give them a hand-up in their times of anxiety and uncertainty. Give strength we pray to the leaders and helpers in the Out of the Cold ministry, in the Meals On Wheels program, at the House of Compassion, and at the Food Bank. We thank you for the sacramental nature of their service to the church and community, as they offer food and drink and counsel to those in need.

We pray, O Lord, for those who are leading the Bible Studies, the Youth programs, and the Sunday morning classes – that in their preparation they will glean truths from your Word that they in turn can pass on to the participants – insights that will help them overcome the temptations of the world and to be understanding and compassionate with others.

We pray, O Lord, that you would be with us as we continue in worship and communion this morning, determined to leave this house of worship confident that your Spirit will provide us with the energy and passion to live in faithful service of our Lord and Saviour Jesus Christ, in whose Name we pray.

Holy, Holy, Holy, Lord God Almighty, it is with awesome wonder that we hear you beckoning us into your Way, where Truth and Life abide. That you should call any of us into your service is an amazing thing, and humbling too. To be your ambassadors of reconciliation in a fractured world is even more astonishing. But it is your Way, and we your servants are so conscious of our need to be assured of your blessing upon what we do in your Name, whether in the church or on the streets of Toronto or in the broader world.

On this beautiful March morning, after a weekend of snow, we come to you the Lord of eternal perspective, thanking you that you help us dig out from all sorts of adversities, and then provide us with continuing opportunities for worship and fellowship, for family time and reflection for work and recreation. We thank you for this church, a refuge from busyness and turmoil – and yet a place where we are stimulated by your Word, and challenged by your Spirit to live out the implications of our commitment to Jesus your Son.

Gracious and merciful God, we thank you for your unconditional love – the love of a holy parent which accepts us as we are, and embraces us with warmth and encouragement. Help those of us who are earthly parents, O God, to be faithful in extending that same love to our children, our spouses, and all around us. We thank you for the example you set, Heavenly Father, that when we stumble and fall, you pick us up, dust us off and continue to give us your affection – a love which forgives and renews and spreads to others. We pray, O Lord, for families in an age when stress is high and time limited: for parents who have to work long hours and yet are also involved in community and church activities while trying to maintain strong family ties; and for children who are super-involved in school and sports and music and part-time jobs; and for grandparents who endeavor to spend time with family in the midst of their own busy lives. At the beginning of March Break, help us all to remember to take the time for each family member, as well as opportunities for relaxation, for reading, for spiritual growth.

O God of mercy and compassion, of comfort and healing, may the tender touch of your Spirit be upon our church family members who live in illness and fear and grief. Bless those in the midst of health concerns and allow them a vision of your hope and peace. Give your guiding hand and compassionate heart also to those in the healing arts – to surgeons and nurses, to family practitioners and counselors, to care givers and therapists – that they may see themselves as doing your work in a hurting world. We pray for your comforting peace to be with the bereaved. May they be aware of our prayerful support.

We thank you, O Giver of Good News, that we have eternal hope through our faith in Jesus. Help us as members of this congregation to be faithful in proclaiming Him as the Light of the world through the ways in which we speak and act, so that others may have their lives enriched by knowing Him as Lord and Friend. In His name we pray.

To you, O God, we offer our praise and adoration and gratitude on this Palm Sunday morning. At the advent of the week that is a reminder of Jesus' journey to the cross, help us to experience the same emotions as our Lord, that we may draw closer to Him, readying ourselves for the ultimate revelation of grace and forgiveness. Though the Maker of all things, you know us and empathize with us because you became one with us through your Son, Jesus Christ, who walked the path of obedience all the way to insult, betrayal and death. Though He was later rejected by those who had cheered Him into Jerusalem, you made Him the cornerstone of new life and raised Him to the highest place of honour.

We confess, O Christ, that though we too make a joyful noise at your coming, we often turn our backs on you when the going gets rough; we hail you with good intentions rather than offer you our whole lives; we promise to follow you wherever you lead, but often we do not. Instead, like Peter, we deny you; we try to fit in with the crowd; we avoid risking ourselves for your sake and for the sake of the gospel. Forgive us, O Lord, for our timid and faltering faith, and for our part in nailing you to the cross to suffer and die. Yet you have opened the gates of justice and become our salvation, so with shouts of "hallelujah" on this Palm Sunday we greet your appearing, and acknowledge your glory in the highest heaven.

As we enter Holy Week and observe the last few days of your life on earth, we thank you for the reminders of your compassionate nature in the Gospels, and for the promise that you remain with us during all the trials and the joys of our journeys. We ask now for your healing and strengthening presence to be with those struggling with health issues, yet we also rejoice over the birth of new children. We ask for your companionship and nourishing presence to be with those who have little shelter and an inadequate diet, yet we are grateful for ministries such as Out of the Cold and House of Compassion. We ask for your reassuring presence and protection in communities where there are high rates of crime and fear, yet we are thankful for law enforcement agencies and organizations such as Youth Unlimited that promote peace and reconciliation. We ask for your consoling presence to be with those whose lives have been torn apart by war, yet we are encouraged by signs of negotiation and peace in some areas of the world.

We thank you, O God, for the presence this morning of our Lieutenant Governor and his wife. We are grateful not only for what they represent – good governance and justice – but also for their example of graciousness and self-sacrificial service in our community and Province.

We thank you, King of Kings and Lord of Lords, for providing us with the faith and the resources to advance the Good News in our city and world, and pray that you would make us brave in helping others to feel the impact of your loving and forgiving Spirit on their lives, for we ask all these things in your Name.

MARCH 20

Good Friday

O Lord and merciful God, on this Friday which was sorrowful for you and yet so good for us, we acknowledge and confess in your presence that it was our sinful nature that is so prone to evil and slothful in good that made your Son's sacrifice on the Cross necessary. You alone know how often we have sinned, wandering from your ways, wasting your gifts, forgetting and even betraying your love. O Lord, have mercy upon us. We are ashamed and sorry for all the ways in which we have caused your displeasure. Yet you love us still. Cleanse us, we pray, from debilitating guilt, and forgive our sins, for the sake of your Son, our Saviour.

Lord, we come to you now with gratitude for your love which enables our forgiveness. As Jesus said from the Cross: "Father, forgive them, for they know not what they do," we thank you that Jesus did as He told others to do, and forgave those who wronged Him. Help us to forgive others from our hearts. And forgive the people of our world, we pray, for still committing acts of great cruelty.

As Jesus said from the Cross: "Truly, I say to you, today you will be with me in Paradise," we thank you that Jesus gave this assurance to a man convinced he deserved to die. Awaken us to a true understanding of what we are and what we have done. But give us, too, the same assurance, that whatever we have done, nothing can separate us from your love.

As Jesus said from the Cross to His mother: "Woman, here is your son," and to John, "Here is your mother," we thank you, Lord, that Jesus thought of others even when dying. Help us to be like Christ to our families and to our neighbours, acting as Jesus would act, mediating your love.

As Jesus said from the Cross: "My God, my God, why have you forsaken me?" We thank you, God, that Jesus was fully human, and no stranger to the anguish of despair. Help us also through the dark times, so that we may emerge with faith strengthened. As Jesus said from the Cross: "I thirst," we thank you that someone answered that cry. Help us to answer the cry of those in our world who are hungry and thirsty, and inspire us to answer their needs.

As Jesus said from the Cross: "It is finished," we thank you, God, that Jesus died knowing He had done your will and accomplished your work. May we too be faithful in laboring in your vineyard, and when we die, lay our deeds before you, the merciful One, with confidence.

As Jesus said from Cross: "Father, into your hands I commit my spirit," we thank you, God, that Jesus died trusting fully in you. May all Christians have the same confidence in the hour of death. May all people know that Jesus has conquered death for us all.

O Lord God, we ask that you would even now send your purifying grace into our hearts that we may continue to live in your light and walk in your ways, for we ask it in the name of Jesus Christ who gave of Himself on the Cross for us.

We come to you with immense gratitude, O God, that you have granted us an Easter faith to celebrate and live and breathe. All of nature celebrates too, soon to be coming out of winter's cold and hibernation, with buds about to appear on trees, and birds from the south arriving back in Canada. All of this is natural and good, but pales in comparison with a man rising from the dead. As we celebrate the resurrection of the Lord Jesus, show us how to truly mark this day – by being people of hope and renewal, eager to pass on to others the good news of your love for all.

We thank you for the implications of Easter, O God. That because Jesus was victorious over sin and death, we can live as forgiven people, free now to use the gifts and abilities you have instilled within us unencumbered with guilt. That because Jesus offered a word of encouragement to Mary outside the empty tomb, we can extend comfort and consolation to those who are in the midst of grief because of the death of a relative or friend. We pray this morning for all who mourn and especially for the families of soldiers killed on the battlefield of Afghanistan and other countries at war.

And we thank you that because Jesus said, "Peace be with you," to the incredulous disciples in the room where they had gathered in fear, we can offer a word of hope to those who think that peace will never come for them. That because Jesus patiently pointed out His own wounds to a doubting Thomas, we can help those who have little faith to meet the One who suffered and died for them too. That because Jesus said to Peter, "Feed my sheep," we can be encouragers, and offer spiritual nourishment and your love to those who would follow Jesus.

We pray, O Lord, for those who are feeling discouraged on this Easter Day, because they are confined to hospital or home or nursing home, isolated from friends and family. To all who are affected by illness, whether patient or family member or colleagues at work, give them, we ask, faith, hope and healing love. We pray that they may feel your peace and strength.

We think this Easter Day, of those who are serving you on the mission field, separated through distance from family and friends. We thank you for your anointing presence with all who minister in the name of Christ, and ask that you would continue to give them encouragement and energy in their discipleship and service.

Help us all, O God, to not simply be observers at this wonderful service of Easter celebration, but to be spiritually moved in such a way that we will leave this house of prayer determined to vigorously live the Easter faith, in the Name of Jesus Christ, our Risen Saviour and Lord.

Almighty God, on this damp morning of spring, we are reminded that you have created anything but a dull world, that what for us is a dreary day of mist and cloud after a night of rain is for you the means by which your earth turns green again, and flowers blossom into colour, and buds and leaves dress the trees. We come to you with thankfulness in our hearts for the perspective that faith brings to our lives – that what may appear to be negative is transformed into hope and renewal. When we see the wonderful signs of your Creation all about us in this season of new life, we thank you that the past never has the last word, that your light can pierce the darkness and that out of deadness comes new life. We pray that the newness that only you can bring may be found in us, transforming us into people of hope.

May your new life transform our sinful natures, O God. When we give in to temptation, yielding to pride and selfishness and greed, remake us, we pray, into the image of Jesus who put other people first, offered forgiveness, and died on the Cross in order that we all may be resurrected to renewed ways of living fruitful and purposeful lives for Him.

May your new life transform our work, O Lord. Often we do our jobs reluctantly or resentfully, and become bound by routine, or forget the usefulness of our work to others, or lose interest in it. Help us to trust that our work has a place in your purpose, and to go about our jobs reliably and enthusiastically. May your new life transform our warring world, O Lord. May hostilities and acts of terror end soon in countries where citizens feel unsafe, their lives and livelihoods threatened. Help them to have faith that leads to hope, through your transforming love.

And may your new life transform our family relationships,

O God. May we honor our mothers, whether in reality or memory, and express gratitude for the positive, nurturing impact they have had on our lives, help us to truly honour them by the way in which we love and support and nurture others, and through always believing in the possibility of reconciliation in our family life.

Creator God, you are always at work bringing new life. Help us, as your faithful followers, to join you in bringing the good news of love and renewal to all those who have never met Jesus Christ, the One we know as Lord and Saviour, for we pray in His Name.

APRIL 5

O Lord God, Creator of all, in this season of new life, open our eyes to greening of the earth, open our ears to the songs of nature, open our minds to the wonders of the universe, open our hearts to you. Through your Spirit, give us a vision, O Lord, to see what we can achieve through your encouragement, to reach out beyond ourselves, to share our lives with others, to stretch our capabilities, to increase our sense of purpose, to be aware of where we can help others, to be sensitive to your presence, to give heed to your constant call. Through your Son, give us freedom, O God, from the selfishness of greed, from the carelessness of apathy, from the temptation of coveting, from the guilt of sin, and encourage us to take advantage of your offer of love and forgiveness.

We pray also for others, O Lord: for those fighting disease and recovering from operations or treatments or therapy, for those saddened by loss and needing comfort or companionship or hope: for those who mourn the passing of loved ones. We pray for those who provide compassion and medical assistance and administrative skills in our hospitals and nursing homes and communities; and for all health care professionals who join Jesus, the Great Physician, in bringing a sense of wholeness to people's lives. May those who suffer from depression and anxiety and various disorders feel the support of family and friends and therapists, and know the peace and hope of your Spirit.

We pray also for those who are destitute and seeking food or employment or housing; for those who are imprisoned and longing for family or purpose or freedom; for those in war zones and hoping for safety or quiet or peace; for those being persecuted for their beliefs and needing encouragement or endurance or enlarged faith. We ask that you would meet these needs, O

God, and help all to feel your comforting presence in their lives. We thank you for the challenge you lay before us in your Word to live out the Gospel on a daily basis. As one of our congregation today enters the waters of baptism, may her witness be an inspiration to all of us to make Jesus known through our words and actions in a world in need of his compassion and forgiveness and hope. May we continue to glory in your presence and further commit ourselves to faithfully serve our Lord and Saviour, Jesus Christ, in whose name we ask all these things.

APRIL 12

Almighty God, on this beautiful morning of bud and bloom, we are reminded of the constant unfolding of your creative work in the world, of your unmatched goodness and of your refreshing love. We confess that we do not think about you enough, let alone talk to you. Forgive us for our neglect, O Lord, even as we begin now to speak to you in prayer.

When we see the wonderful signs of your creation all about us in this season of new life, how can we not express our gratitude? But it is when we remember past times when things were not so wonderful for us that we have doubts – when we were sick and in pain or when we were in trouble and distress and sorrow. We thank you, though, that the past never has the last word, that your light can pierce the darkness and that out of deadness comes new life. We pray that the newness that only you can bring may be found in us, transforming us into people of hope.

May your new life transform our work, O Lord. Often we do our jobs reluctantly or resentfully, and become bound by routine, or forget the usefulness of our work to others, or lose interest in it. Help us to trust that our work and our voluntary endeavors have a place in your purpose, and to go about our jobs reliably and enthusiastically.

May your new life transform our neighborhoods, O God. We often fail to get to know our neighbours, and then blame them because we feel lonely and neglected. Help us to overcome the shyness and hesitation which holds us back from getting to know people, and to offer compassionate friendship to others.

May your new life transform our family relationships, O God. We can become estranged from members of the family at home; or we offend relatives, and drift away from them, and then we are afraid to write a letter or call on them for fear of being rejected. Help us always to believe in the possibility of reconciliation in our family life.

May your new life transform our fears, O Lord. When we are suddenly confronted with illness or accident, or the threat of disease, help us to put our trust in your Son the Great Physician and in your Spirit the Great Comforter. We ask for your healing love to be with those who suffer through the difficult times of pain and worry.

May your new life transform our warring world, O Lord. May hostilities and acts of terror end soon in countries where citizens feel unsafe, their lives and livelihoods threatened. Help them to have faith that leads to hope, through your transforming peace.

Creator God, you are always at work bringing new life. Help us, as your faithful followers, to join you in bringing the good news of love and renewal to all we encounter on a daily basis. May our offering of adoration this morning bring glory and honour to your Name, for we ask these things through Jesus Christ, the One we know as Lord and Redeemer.

APRIL 19

Almighty God, Creator of the world in which we live and work, and builder of the Church in which we worship and serve, we come to praise your Name, to sing your glory, to absorb your Word, and to seek your guiding Spirit. With gratitude we celebrate the impact you have on our lives in revealing your loving and forgiving nature through your Son Jesus, the Light of the World. We acknowledge, however, our tendency to disobedience and our giving in to temptation. As we confess our sins before you now in silence, we pray for your forgiving grace and mercy.

As well as pardon for our sins, we ask for help in resisting further temptation: deliver us from the tendency to build ourselves up while tearing others down; free us from pride that prevents us from admitting mistakes; give us courage to seek forgiveness of others; keep us in a state of peace of mind that we may convey your peace to others.

Be with those, we pray, who are feeling trapped: those who are trapped in poverty and joblessness; or in an occupation with low wages and little development of skills; in families where there is little love; in addictions and low self-esteem; in worry and depression. Help them through faith in you to be freed from all that restrains them and to know joy in life.

We bring to you the members of our families and congregation who are ill and bereaved. May your healing touch be felt by all in need of your soft hand upon their shoulder.

Our thoughts and prayers turn to the many millions in the Sudan and Iraq and Afghanistan affected by civil war. May their hope for peace be eventually realized through the curtailing of infighting amongst the warlords and more stable governments in their lands. For those affected by floods on the one hand and drought on the other, we ask that they will be encouraged by the generosity of people of faith who provide relief agencies with food and supplies to meet their needs.

We pray also for the homeless and hungry on the streets of Toronto. May our efforts through the Food Banks and Youth Unlimited demonstrate our concern for them in your Name.

We thank you, O Lord, for those who volunteer on the boards and committees and groups of this congregation, and for the generosity of your people who are committed to supporting the work of Christ in our church and community and broader world. May your Spirit give us light on how we can continue to serve you faithfully and wisely through the vision and gifts and skills you have instilled within us.

Help us all, O God, to not simply be observers of the ministry you have given us, but to be spiritually moved in our worship in such a way that we will leave this house of prayer determined to vigorously live the resurrection faith, in the Name of Jesus Christ, our Saviour and Lord.

APRIL 26

O Lord of heaven and earth, Maker of stars and of atoms, of insects and of people, we approach you now in reverence and praise, full of wonder that you should love us. Yet we experience that love through all of the material benefits we enjoy, through the companionship of family members and friends, through the pleasure of our senses and the beauty and bounty of your earth, but above all, we feel your love through the free gift of forgiveness – freeing for us, O God, but of enormous sacrifice for you. We are grateful that you came to us through Jesus your Son, who died on the Cross for us, setting us free from guilt, and assuring our eternal future with you.

We come to you through Jesus the Great Physician, asking for healing mercies to be with members of our congregation and community who are full of anxiety, experiencing pain, awaiting medical procedures, undergoing therapy. May they feel the wholeness of your presence and the prayerful support of your people.

We come to you through Jesus the Great Comforter, asking for your consoling presence to be with those who continue to feel the shock and loneliness months and years after losing family members and friends.

We come to you through Jesus the Great Shepherd, asking for your protection with the children and the innocents of society, your consolation with the victims of crime and prejudice, your assurance with the homeless and impoverished, and your hope with the unemployed.

We come to you through Jesus the Prince of Peace, asking for your intervention in the Sudan where thousands are dying of ethnic cleansing and starvation, in Afghanistan and Iraq where people are terrified of bombs and kidnapers, in Israel and Palestine and Lebanon where there is such instability and civil strife, in North Korea where there is terrible poverty and lack of freedom. May those who have political influence act out of compassion and a sense of justice rather than power and self-interest. Work through the United Nations and relief organizations and churches, we pray, to bring security and food and hope to those caught up in war and poverty and persecution.

We come to you through Jesus the Light of the World, asking for your presence with missionaries and chaplains and seminary professors and ministers who have been commissioned by your Spirit to proclaim the Gospel in such a way that people will see you as the light of their lives, no longer having to live in guilt and fear and uncertainty.

We come to you through Jesus the Way, the Truth and the Life, asking for your guidance and encouragement and spiritual energy to be with us all as we continue to grow in our relationship with Him, your Son and our Saviour and Lord, in whose Name we pray.

MAY 3

Almighty Creator God, who brought all things from a formless void of darkness into wondrous light, and whose steadfast love is from everlasting to everlasting, we approach you now as a child does a loving parent, with trust and confidence; but also with an open hand, pleading for your gifts, while acknowledging that we are already spoiled by your generosity.

First, in humility, we ask for your forgiveness. We often act like spoiled children, overindulging in things that entice us away from your Spirit and lead us back into sin's darkness. In the Name of Jesus, who died for us, we ask you take the accumulated guilt away and free us to be mature people who live in the light, who are pure in heart, who are honest with ourselves and others, and who emulate your generosity.

We pray, O loving and compassionate God, for those who are going through times of great stress: the homeless and the lonely, the despised and the hungry, the misjudged and the imprisoned, the suffering and the dying. Help us to abandon preoccupation with our own needs in order to be like Jesus who gave of Himself, fed the hungry, and offered hope and cure. We ask for your healing Spirit to be with the ill that they may feel your soothing support.

We pray, O God of peace, for those who are affected by war and civil strife and terrorism: the children who are now parentless, the parents who are now childless; those whose homes are destroyed and have lost their livelihood; the victims of prejudice and genocide; the wounded and traumatized. We pray for your Spirit to be influential in the cause for peace; and that those who fight over religious issues in places throughout the world may learn to be tolerant and peaceful. We ask, too, for your Spirit of calmness to prevail over the land-claims disputes with Aboriginal peoples – that the issues will be resolved without further inflammatory language and violence.

We pray, O God, for those involved in mission, who endeavor to bring good news of your love and forgiveness to those who do not know you, the Lord of Life. May their Christian demeanor and friendly personalities overcome differences in language and culture, enabling them to be your faithful disciples.

As we continue in our worship this morning, O Lord, give us a thirst for a better understanding of your Word and of how it can impact directly upon our lives. We thank you for the ways you have used the gifts and personalities of members of this congregation over the years to enhance the lives of others through the power of your Spirit and to be effective servants and witnesses of Christ in the surrounding community. We pray for continued visionary leadership from your Spirit, that we may be a welcoming community of faith, using our resources and spiritual gifts for your honour and glory. Encourage us all to be your effective servants through the way in which we treat with kindness those around us, and demonstrate that we belong to you, the Lord of life and love, for we pray in the Name of Jesus Christ, our Saviour and Friend.

Almighty God, Creator of all, when we contemplate the vastness of the universe, and the length of time it has existed, and
try to imagine the purpose for which you created it, we confess
that we are, like the scientists, simply amazed. Yet we believe
you have a purpose, revealed through the Scriptures and
through the ministry of your Son Jesus. A purpose motivated by
love, a love that you would have us pass on to others. We are
reminded that our individual lives become complete as we live
in community, particularly in the community of your church.
We thank you that together we can do so much more good than
we can do separately; yet we confess that together we also do
evil things we should never dream of doing as individuals. We
exclude some from our community life for selfish and unworthy
reasons; we ignore others because no one draws attention to
their needs; we force yet others to turn their backs on the
church through our false piety and indifference. We confess
these things, O Lord, and pray that through the miracle of
forgiveness you would set us free from our imperfect past and
re-make us in the image of Christ.

How we thank you that we know you through Jesus the
Great Physician, the One who healed in body, mind and spirit
those who were burdened with illness, the One who brought
comfort and consolation to the bereaved, and the One who fed
those who were hungry in body and soul. As we pause for a
moment in silence to bring to you those whom we know in need
of healing strength, we ask for your comforting presence to be
with them.

Help us, also, O God, to be your agents of compassion in
our community. May we bring reassurance to those who live in

fear, companionship to those who are lonely, guidance to those who feel lost in a confusing world, and hope to those overwhelmed with work and family responsibilities.

We pray, too, O Lord, for those who are caught up in war, the innocent people who are affected by bombs and embargoes and land mines, that you would give them your protection. Help the leaders of the nations to make decisions that will lead to peace rather than hostility, and inspire us all to be peacemakers through the way in which we treat one another.

Again we thank you, O God, that we know you through Jesus, who became one of us, identifies and empathizes with us, and encourages us through the power of the Spirit to bring the wonderful good news of your offer of salvation to all around us, for we ask these things in His Name. Amen.

Almighty God, Creator of all that lives, Maker of all that breathes, Source of all that grows, nothing can exist apart from you. On this May weekend, as we see life unfolding in leaf and blossom and nest, we are so grateful that we can talk to the One who started it all and sustains all. We ask for your blessing on the land and those who work it in this planting season. Give safety and energy to farmers and gardeners who labour to nourish your people and feed the nations. Bless, O Lord, those who are advocates for the air, the land, the sea, and all endangered creatures, and help each of us, who are consumers, to also be good stewards. Encourage us to be sharing, generous people – to give unselfishly to food banks at home and relief agencies abroad, so that none of your people will go to their beds hungry. We pray also for organizations such as Habitat For Humanity, who make it possible for families to own their own home through a hand-up gesture of support, and ask that staff and volunteers and suppliers will have the energy and the resources they need to continue this important ministry in Toronto and abroad.

We ask for your consoling presence to be with the millions of people in China affected by the earthquakes. May those who remain trapped in the rubble be rescued soon and restored to their families. We feel deeply, O Lord, for those in Burma/ Myanmar awaiting food and water that is available just offshore. Soften the hearts of the political leaders that relief efforts will allowed to reach the people in need.

We come to you now asking for your stabilizing presence to be with those whose lives have been shattered and turned upside down by illness, or grief or the breakdown of a relationship. Give your Spirit of wholeness to them in their times of discomfort, and your consoling Spirit to be with all who are suffering sorrow; and your reconciling Spirit to those who are distraught over a dispute with a friend or family member.

We who seek peace within ourselves and for others come to you, the Author of peace, through your forgiveness, justice, hope and love. Be with the family and colleagues of soldiers who have lost their lives in Afghanistan and Iraq while trying to establish peace, and with civilians mourning the death of loved ones in terrible civil wars.

On this weekend set apart to honour a long-ago Queen, we pray for all those who continue to rule over us: our Queen Elizabeth, our Prime Minister, our Premier, our Mayor and all politicians and government officials. We thank you for the leadership of these individuals, who are given the responsibility of legislating and decision making, and who give generously of their time and commitment for the governing of us all. We ask that you would give them wisdom in their deliberations, compassion in their dealings with individuals, and calmness under the pressures they face from all sides of a given issue. We pray for us, the citizens whom they govern, that we may be prayerfully supportive of our political leaders, whether in agreement with their decisions or not, and continue to honour the gift of the democratic process. We do thank you, O God, for the freedom of conscience and of vote in this privileged land of Canada. Above all help us to be faithful to you, the Ruler of all. We realize, O Lord, that if we prayed in pure faith that mountains of strife would crumble, and that the power of your Holy Spirit would be a force for peace that every person could feel and act upon. So we ask for the enlightenment of your truth, that our doubts may vanish, and that the distribution of your love through us might be felt by those around us. We thank you for the hope and the promise that this is possible through the redeeming presence and power of your Son Jesus Christ, whom we know as Saviour and Lord, and in whose Name we pray.

MAY 24

Almighty God, you who are the Creator of the cosmos, yet the Saviour and Comforter of each of us, we are reminded as we approach you in prayer of your perfect wisdom and goodness, of your unbounded love, and of your compassionate understanding. We have so much to be thankful for, O God: for the good life of comfort and security that most of us experience, for the love of family and friends, for the opportunities of using our talents, and above all, for the clemency and forgiveness made available to us through Jesus your Son. As we pause for a moment to confess our individual sins to you, hear us, we pray with ears of mercy, and forgive us of our trespasses.

Even as we are assured of your forgiveness, O Lord, we approach you also in petition. We pray for those who are ill and in pain and full of anxiety. Be with them in their suffering and allow them to experience your soothing touch. We pray for those who are caring for elderly or disabled relatives, that you would give them energy and patience to match their compassion. We pray for those who are required to work outdoors, for farmers and construction workers and maintenance people and fire fighters, that they will have stamina under difficult conditions. We pray for those travelling this weekend, that they will have safety on the roads and in the air, and a sense of renewal through times of relaxation.

Even as we live in relative peace and safety in this land and city, we are aware of areas of your world where there is conflict and fear. We pray for the people of Afghanistan and of Lebanon and of Iraq who are experiencing civil wars. We think especially of our Canadian Baptist Ministry workers in Beirut. Give them safety and courage as they provide food and assistance to dozens of families in their war-torn region. Give comfort, we pray, to the thousands of people mourning the loss of relatives, and living in fear for their own lives. We also ask for the influence of your Spirit upon the minds and hearts of political and military leaders, that they will find ways to end the hostilities and bring peace to their lands.

Help us, we pray, O God, to be aware of our own failings when it comes to fostering reconciliation. Enable us to be less critical, to offer words of encouragement, to be full of love, to bring joy to others, and to exemplify the character of Jesus in all of our relationships, for all of these things we ask in His Name.

Pentecost

Almighty God, Lord of all, whose Spirit swept over the face of the waters on the day of Creation, we come to you with gratitude on this Pentecost Sunday that you have breathed new life into us – into your Church. We have felt the wonder of your Spirit come to fullness within us – and we celebrate it today, along with an appreciation for the depth of your love and for all the gifts of the Spirit you have instilled with us.

We confess to you, though, that we have not been as faithful to you as we should in imparting your love to others or in using the gifts of the Spirit wisely, and admit to all of the ways in which we hurt others through the disobedience of your commands. And so we ask for your forgiveness and that you would, "Breathe on us, Breath of God."

O God – we pray for the blowing of your Holy Spirit upon all who are in need of healing, whether of body, or of mind, or of spirit. Rescue those who are dead in hope and in heart and give them, we pray, the will to endure along with an experience of your renewal and peace. We pray this morning for those among us who are ill, and also for those in grief over the loss of loved ones.

We ask also, O Lord, that your Spirit of encouragement would be with those who lack adequate shelter and food and employment, and with families who are struggling to make ends meet. We thank you for organizations like Youth Unlimited and Yonge St. Mission and House of Compassion and Habitat for Humanity, and for those of our congregation who provide counsel and support through these ministries.

We thank you, O God, for the willingness of missionaries to leave comfortable surroundings and family, and travel to other countries in order to introduce people to a faith that proclaims freedom of conscience and justice and love and life everlasting, prompting them to say: "Breathe on us, Breath of God."

Again we thank you, O God, for the inspiration of your Holy Spirit, and ask that you would help us in your church to use wisely the power you have granted to us and to share it with others, so that blessing and wholeness may come upon all, for we ask these things in Jesus' name.

SUMMER

JUNE 7
Service in the Park

Almighty God, Creator of all that lives, Maker of all that breathes, Source of all that grows, nothing can exist apart from you. On this warm June evening, as we see life displayed in leaf and bloom and wing, we are so grateful that we can talk to the One who started it all and sustains all. We ask for your blessing on the land and those who work it in this summer season. Give safety and energy to farmers and gardeners who labour to nourish your people and feed the nations. Bless, O Lord, those who are advocates for the air, the land, the sea, and all endangered creatures, and help each of us, who are consumers, to also be good stewards. Encourage us to be sharing, generous people – to give unselfishly to food banks at home and relief agencies abroad, so that none of your people will go to their beds hungry tonight.

We come to you with gratitude for your amazing, forgiving grace, O Lord. We confess that we take the abundance of your earth, the love of family, the companionship of friends, the beauty around us for granted, and often misuse our gifts and abilities. We ask that you would remake us to be like Jesus, who, though tempted as we are, rejected devilish impulses and made Himself available for your service.

We thank you for the miracle of sound, O God. That breath through brass can create such beauty through music to make our feet stomp and our hearts soar is a wonder to us, but we rejoice in the talent of musicians and the gift of hearing. As we sound your praises through instrument and voice in this park this evening, inspire us to proclaim your good news in all the neighbourhoods in which we live.

May the gentle wind of your Spirit blow upon our lives, O

Lord, cooling our angers, refreshing our faith, lifting our hopes, directing our vision that we may be effective witnesses of Jesus Christ, our Saviour and Friend, in whose Name we pray. Amen.

JUNE 14

Almighty God, we acknowledge you as the One who has ultimate power and strength. All that we see and have was created by you. Also from you comes the love that forgives, the justice that heals, the power that sustains, and the word that leads to joy and peace. You are our source of comfort and eternal hope. You sent Jesus into the world to be the Light of the world. We pray that you would help us now to see the light of hope in the midst of desperate times in the world. Fill us with faith that we might trust in your never-ending love, your boundless grace, and your power to save us.

Lord you call us to follow you – to be your disciples – and you call us to make disciples of others – to be ambassadors of Christ; to share your reconciling love with our neighbours; to be proclaimers of your Gospel. But we confess that we are often like Jonah, slow to acknowledge our prejudices, running away from our responsibilities, and ignoring your instructions. So we ask that you would forgive us of our sins, and strengthen us in our calling. Help us to be disciplined in our daily practice of devotion, prayer, and meditation. Help us to avail ourselves of the nourishment you provide us day by day through your Word that we may be the new creation that you desire us to be.

Help us, O Lord, to be faithful to the words of Jesus who prayed that we might be one in our devotion to Him. Draw us closer to you and to our brothers and sisters in Christ Jesus that we may better know your will and work cooperatively together that others might experience the fullness of your grace. We ask for your healing grace to be with any who are going through the dark times of illness and pain and grief.

Help us also, O Lord, to work together for issues of justice and peace when we see the world in its darkness. Help us to know what to do, what to say, and how to say it, so the leaders of the nations will hear and respond. When we see abuses of power and wealth, help us to be examples of humility and generosity. When we see epidemic diseases such as AIDS, help us to support those who are your healing agents. When we see poverty, help us to enrich others. Enable us, we pray, to reflect the life of Jesus in the ways in which we promote peace and help the people of the world to know that nothing can ever separate us from your love.

We thank you that our faith is like a towering maple, offering shelter and shade and majestic beauty to our lives. We acknowledge that, unlike the trees of nature, your shelter of protection does not age, is not finite, is not subject to disease and rot, does not fall apart, cannot be cut down. Yours is an everlasting haven within which we feel secure and nurtured and loved, knowing that it is upon your Spirit that we depend.

We thank you, O God, for being attentive to all of our prayers, for we ask all of these things in Jesus' Name, and for the sake of your Church. Amen.

Almighty God, Creator of all and Lord of each of us, to whom every heart is open and every secret known, we worship and praise you, the One whose hands moulded us, whose mouth breathed life into us, whose eyes are watching over us and whose ears are open to our cries. We approach you with great reverence, but also with the confidence of children who speak to a loving Parent.

We come humbly, asking that in your great mercy you would forgive our sins. We are rightly burdened with guilt, with the memory of failure and with the bonds of sinful habit. Although we have been immensely blessed by you, we have been ungrateful; although trusted, we have been disloyal, though forgiven, we have been unforgiving. Free us, we pray, of all that would hinder us from being your faithful servants. As we read in your Word of how Jesus was patient with His disciples, grant us patience to bear with other people's faults, humbly remembering our own, to accept life's disappointments with grace, and to faithfully serve you through the abilities you have instilled within us.

As Jesus relieved the suffering of the people of His day, make your presence known to those who suffer from various diseases, or disabilities or nervous disorders. As we fear the outbreak of epidemic diseases in this city, we ask that you would be with the health care professionals as they endeavour to find ways to keep them under control. Bring your healing presence to those already affected by pneumonia and communicable illnesses, and support and relieve them, we pray, through the skill of doctors, the care of nurses and the sympathy of friends; and allow the assurance of your love and concern to bring comfort to family members who are unable to visit patients. We ask also, O Lord, that you would bring hope to all who are battling against the terrible pandemic of HIV/AIDS in the world. Prompt the governments and charitable foundations and pharmaceutical companies to contribute adequate funds to relieve the suffering of millions and develop a cure of this awful disease.

To you, O God, we commend our hurting world, asking that we in your church will have the energy and the courage to fight against evil, strive for peace and encourage compassion. Deliver us into your care and keeping this day, for we pray in the Name of Jesus, our Saviour and Lord.

JUNE 28
Canada Day

In awe and wonder and praise, we approach you now, O God, asking for your presence through our evening prayer. We thank you for this building in which we worship. A house made with hands, yet which fosters faith and devotion eternal in the heavens; a shelter from the storms of nature and the storms of life; a sanctuary in which we lift our voices in joyful song and our souls in heartfelt adoration. Even as we gather within these walls, we ask in the name of Jesus that you would break down other walls – walls of separation and division, walls of hostility and prejudice. Help us to be a welcoming faith community where others may experience peace, wholeness, and healthy relationships. Help us to see how all people are our sisters and brothers, no matter where they come from or what they have done in the past, no matter what the differences are in how they dress or act or earn their living, no matter how varied the way may be in how they worship you and call upon your name. Give us the eyes of Christ – and place within us His heart of compassion, His mind of truth, His words of wisdom and His acts of justice. Remind us that your Spirit is at work in all our relationships and grant us trust and faith in your power to overcome those things which keep us apart.

We pray, O God, for all in this congregation and community who are experiencing anxiety or illness or grief in their lives. May they be comforted by your renewing, strengthening grace, and by our visits and cards and listening ears. We pray for all who are bowed down by guilt or emotional pain and who see nothing in their future but fear and loneliness – may they experience your loving forgiveness, the hope of faith, and the support of family and friends.

We bring to you now all who are involved in mission, whether at home or overseas. Give them safety in the face of threats and prejudice, endurance in the heat of tropical countries, and courage in proclaiming your Word faithfully.

We thank you, O Lord, for our country of Canada. As we celebrate, this day, make us determined to exercise our freedom in ways that will build others up, demonstrating compassion, courage, faith, discipline, trust in you, and the love for one another that will be a witness to the world that we are a nation under your guidance and blessing. We ask that you would be with our political leaders in all levels of government. Give them wisdom in decision making, integrity in governing, compassion for the people, and energy to sustain them in meetings and in relating to constituents.

We ask all of these things in the Name of Jesus Christ, the Saviour of the world. Amen.

JULY 5

Eternal God, Creator of all, we call upon you now through the great gift of prayer, with praise on our lips and joy in our hearts as we are reminded in this summer season of the brightness and beauty and bounty of your Creation. We so appreciate the fresh taste of garden produce, the bright colours of the flowers, the refreshing walks in the evenings, the hearty laughter of friends at a barbeque. And we thank you for the opportunity – the privilege – of worship, as we put all the worry and hurts and bitterness behind us for an hour in order to glory in your presence. Lift us above our doubts and complaints and feelings of inadequacy so that we might enjoy the peace of your presence. Free us from guilt too, we pray. Though we are well-deserving of shame because of our sin, we appeal to you in the Name of Jesus for forgiveness. Renew our spirits that we might be more energetic in our proclamation of Jesus as the Saviour of the world. We thank you, O God, for the members of our families and for those who stand beside us when we are in trouble or in sickness or in sorrow. We pray for those who are in hospitals, and for those who are awaiting operations, and thank you for the skill of doctors and nurses and technicians who bring relief and hope to those who are suffering. As we think of our suffering brothers and sisters this evening, may they be aware of the support of your Spirit.

We think, too, O Lord, of the suffering of millions of people in countries where there is famine and disease and political instability. We thank you that your Spirit is prompting relief agencies and medical personnel and peace keepers to give aid and healing and security in areas where there is so much turmoil. Help us to demonstrate our Christian compassion by being generous in support of charitable efforts which offer aid to those who are starving and dying.

We bring to you now all who are involved in mission enterprises throughout the world, that with boldness, yet sensitivity, they might be able to help people find freedom from fear and new meaning in life through a strong relationship with Jesus our Saviour. Be with the many missionaries who are on holiday, perhaps being reunited with children and other family members after months of separation. May they feel renewed in body and in spirit.

And now, O Lord, we ask for your renewing presence in our worship. May we be spiritually refreshed in such a way this evening that we will leave this place more committed to be your dynamic servants in our own city and communities, for we pray in the Name of Jesus, our Lord and Saviour, Amen.

JULY 12

Lord of Creation and of mercy and of love, how grateful we are
for your provision, your forgiveness and your care. We see the
results of your creative Spirit all around us in this summer season
with landscapes of infinite colour and fields of ripening grain
and lakes of shimmering blue. People are enjoying weddings and
picnics and street parties and festivals. We thank you for
reunions of old friends and family members, for conversation
and laughter. You make life enjoyable and challenging and full of
companionship. Forgive us for messing it up with a careless
word, a selfish gesture, a craving thought. We confess that we
too often give in to temptation and damage relationships and
build up layers of guilt. We thank you for your forgiving mercy,
for wiping our corrupted files clean, for renewing our connections with you and others – all made possible through Jesus
Christ who took our place on the guilty line and put us on
another path, to eternal life with you.

We thank you for your Word, whose truths we are able to
read and apply to our lives in this free country of Canada. We
are grateful for the stories and parables of Jesus, who gave us
guidelines for living and relationship building, who provides us
with motivation for charitable giving and hands-on service, and
who not only renewed people in body, mind and spirit in His
day, but passed on the healing arts to doctors and nurses and
therapists of today. We ask for your soothing touch to be with
those suffering from illness and discomfort. We ask for your
comforting Spirit to be with the bereaved, especially the grieving
families of soldiers killed in Afghanistan. We pray for peace in
that land, and in Israel-Palestine and Sudan-Darfur, and Sri
Lanka, where civil war divides neighbours and even families.

Give them hope with substance, we pray, O Lord.

We are conscious of the needs of people in our own city, in neighbourhoods where there is racial tension and crime, and streets where there are homeless youth and adults, and homes where there is drug abuse and violence. We thank you that your Spirit is present there, too, in church congregations who are addressing these issues, in shelters providing food and lodging, and through individual Christians offering a bright smile and an encouraging word and a nourishing sandwich. Help us to see that we are all part of the same community, and thus to care for one another.

We are thankful for this time of worship when we can think about these things through the perspective of faith, and bring to you all of our concerns, as well as our expressions of gratitude. May we be attentive to your leading in all areas of our lives, and give you the honour and glory in all that is said and done, through Jesus Christ our Lord, Amen.

In the midst of a beautiful summer weekend, we come to you, O Lord, with gratitude for moments of companionship with family members and friends, for relaxing times with a good book, for a casual drive in the countryside, for street festivals and theatre, for gardening produce and flowering pots. Along with the song birds we sing your praises for all the pleasures of nature – the sights and sounds of a busy but beautiful world. We thank you for the privilege we have of being part of a larger family this morning – your Church – where we can feel a sense of belonging while offering praise to you through music and prayer, and receive instructions for life through your Word of truth and light.

We come also with gratitude for your forgiving nature, which we are desperately in need of. We confess that we contribute to the despoiling of nature through our polluting and wasteful lifestyles; that we discourage other people through unnecessary criticism and unrealistic expectations; that we harm ourselves in giving in to temptations to overindulge; that we deprive people of a fuller life by not sharing with them the good news of Jesus Christ. Forgive us, we pray, for all behaviours and thoughts that lead us away from you; free us from the guilt, that we can live our lives unencumbered by the past, under the guidance of your Spirit.

We come to you in the Name of Jesus the Great Physician – the One who brings a sense of wholeness to body, mind and spirit. May those who are ill feel your soothing touch upon their lives, and be encouraged by the care of doctors and the thoughts and prayers of family and friends.

We pray for those who live in fear because of suicide

bombers and kidnappers and rifle fire in war-torn regions of the world, and violence and crime in the neighbourhoods of our own city. Give safety to soldiers who are endeavoring to bring peace and to police officers who offer protection in the streets. We thank you for those who offer shelter and food and a kind word to those who do not have a home to call their own, and pray for workers and volunteers with the Light Patrol and with Yonge St. Mission and with various food banks. We ask you to be with the staff at House of Compassion, and at L'Arche and with those struggling through mental health issues.

And now, as we continue in worship of you our Creator and Lord, we pray that you would open our minds to your truth through the Scriptures and the proclamation of the good news, opening our hearts to receive the blessings of your love, that we in turn can pass it on to others that they too might experience your grace, through Jesus Christ our Saviour. Amen.

Almighty God, in whose honour the Psalmist said, "Give unto the Lord, O people, give unto the Lord the glory due His Name (Ps. 29:1-2)," we come before you now in humility, but full of confidence that you hear our prayers, and that you respond in mercy. We come full of praise that you have revealed yourself to us through Jesus your Son, whose life reflected the noble themes we find in your Word: justice and forgiveness, healing and renewal, love and mercy. We thank you that through our faith in Jesus we are still recipients of these gifts.

We confess to you now that we do not pass on these gifts to others in full measure as we should. We often make decisions based on selfishness rather than justice, on revenge rather than forgiveness; our words often cause pain rather than healing, discouragement rather than renewal; and our actions towards others reveal our prejudices rather than love, and blame rather than mercy. In the words of King David, who also sinned, we pray, "Wash us thoroughly from our iniquity and cleanse us from our sins (Ps. 51:2)." We ask this in the Name of Jesus, whose sacrifice on the Cross enabled our forgiveness.

We bring to you now, O Lord, those who are suffering in the hospital or at home; those who are awaiting test results or therapy; and those who are suffering chronic pain. Give them healing and strength and hope. We pray also for those working towards the prevention and cure of the terrible pandemic of HIV-AIDS. May the resources provided by charitable foundations and governments, and the skill of medical researchers, and the compassion of physicians and nurses and caregivers bring hope to those who are suffering, and to their families.

We also come to you in the Name of Jesus the Comforter,

and ask that you would give your consoling Spirit to the relatives and friends and colleagues of those who have died through accident or disease or age, and enable those who are grieving to feel the support of others and the solace of faith.

We appeal to you also in the Name of Jesus the Great Shepherd, asking for protection and restoration for the vulnerable of our city: for teenagers living on the street trying to deal with the pain of past abuse and live in safety in the present; for the unemployed who are endeavoring to support themselves and families with little income; for those with addictions attempting desperately to cope with life; for ex-prisoners yearning again for an accepting community; for Aboriginal Peoples seeking justice. May we, as the Body of Christ in the world, be supportive of them and of those who work most effectively among them, in order to bring the hope of faith to their situations.

We ask tonight that through him "your love may overflow more and more with knowledge and full insight" (Philip. 1:9), and so challenge us to produce a "harvest of righteousness" for the benefit of those who do not yet know you through Jesus the Messiah, in whose Name we have prayed. Amen.

Almighty and everlasting God, we come before you in humility this morning, realizing that we can talk to you about all things, feeling total acceptance. We have a deep desire to express praise and gratitude to you the Creator of all that is good. Thank you for beauty to behold with our eyes, sounds that bring delight to the ear, smells and tastes of the earth's bounty in summer, the touch and embrace of a spouse or friend, minds that can think and reason, talent that fulfills potential, faith that allows hope to develop, and spirits that soar at the very thought of Christ our risen Saviour.

But we also have a need for confession, O God. We know that you do not condemn our limitations and weaknesses, but are saddened by our yielding to temptation, by our excuses, by the hurt we inflict on others, by our laziness in faith and action. We acknowledge our sins, both secret and obvious, and ask for your pardoning grace in the Name of Christ our forgiving Saviour.

We have a need for healing, O God. We are grateful that you work through doctors, nurses, technicians, and medicines to foster the curing of the body and mind, and ask that you would give them energy and expertise as they do your work of healing in the Name of Christ the Great Physician. We pray today that the sick may be aware of the soothing touch of your Spirit and the support of their friends here. We also ask for your comfort to be with family members and friends suffering grief over the death of loved ones. May they feel hope and peace within their souls. We ask for safety for the Koreans who have been kid-napped in Afghanistan – that their faith will give them courage and hope in a desperate situation of fear, and we pray that they will be released soon to their families.

We bring to you those affected by floods in England and various other parts of the world, asking that through the support of community and relief efforts that their homes and their livelihoods will be restored.

We have a need for guidance, O Lord. You have instilled various gifts and abilities within us – help us to use them wisely in order to enhance the lives of others. We thank you for the workers of Light Patrol, who offer food and a listening ear and a word of hope to the youth of Toronto who have to find shelter wherever they can.

We thank you for this sanctuary in which we worship, and for the opportunity to be built up in faith and hope and love. May we leave your house of prayer this morning with a firm commitment to make your presence felt to all we encounter this week, for we ask these things in the Name of Jesus Christ, our risen Saviour and Lord. Amen.

AUGUST 9

Lord God Almighty, we come to you in prayer humbly, yet full of confidence that you listen to your children when we approach your throne of grace. Direct our minds to yourself now, we pray, so that we may speak with assurance and listen with hope. We come to you in the name of your Son, Jesus Christ, through whom all things were created and are held together. We thank you for the great gift of knowing Him, in whose life and death and resurrection your love is perfectly made known. We thank you that Jesus' greatness was exercised in service, even to the furthest point of self sacrifice.

We confess that we fall far short of our potential in living the Christian life. Forgive us, we pray, for our willful disobedience – for the times we have broken your commandments. We deserve the guilt we feel. It's beyond our comprehension that you offer us forgiveness, yet we know you do, because Jesus shed His blood for us. Thank you, Lord, for setting us free; help us to use our freedom in responsible ways – to control our selfish tendencies, and to develop the gifts you have instilled within us by using them in service to you and others.

We ask, O Lord, that your Spirit would be with those who need your healing touch, with children, women and men who are ill, whether in hospital or at home. May they be aware of your comfort and inner peace even in the midst of their discomfort and anxiety.

For those suffering and dying because of the terrible scourge of HIV-AIDS in so many countries of the world, we ask for your mercy. Be with the health and research personnel as they endeavor to fight the disease and find a cure; and give energy and compassion to all working with the relief agencies.

May we do our part in supporting the efforts of The Sharing Way and The Guardians of Hope, and in so doing, act in the Name of Jesus.

We pray also for innocent people caught up in the various conflicts raging in your world, whether in Afghanistan or Iraq or Lebanon or Israel or Sudan. Give them hope for the end of hostilities and for stability in their lands. May those who are injured and those who are grieving know your comforting peace.

How we thank you, O God, that we know you as the Lord of Creation and of History, and for the great privilege we have of making you known to those around us. May we be faithful in our task of introducing to our friends the One who said, "Come to me, all who are weak and heavy laden, and I will give you rest." For we ask it in Jesus' Name. Amen.

AUGUST 16

Eternal God, as we gather to pray to you the Creator and consider the multifaceted universe in which we dwell – when we calm our hearts and our minds in your presence, we are filled with awe and wonder. We sense your Spirit gathering about us, brooding over us, reaching out to us. In the serenity of worship, O Lord, your voice becomes clear to us. We reflect on how it brings fullness of life to us – and how it is good for our souls to hear and respond to your Word. Today, Gracious God, we pray that we might truly sense the wonder of who you are and what you have done and are still doing – and we pray that in this and in all that we do we may bless your Holy Name and be united with you and our brothers and sisters in a holy love.

We acknowledge that we need your love, O God, for there are too many ways in which we are not faithful in listening to your voice, or heeding your Word, or showing compassion to one another. We confess that we often think more highly of ourselves than others; we are selfish and boastful and lustful; we are often unconcerned when people are unemployed or ill or poor or in prison. We confess these sins and ask for your merciful forgiveness. We echo with King David the hope that you would "Create in us a clean heart and put a new and right spirit with us. Restore to us the joy of your salvation, and sustain in us a willing spirit," according to your Word.

Our hearts are heavy, O Lord, and our eyes are saddened from watching the bombing of Iraq. In the midst of war it is difficult for us to sort out the conflicting emotions flooding through our souls. We want the hostilities to end quickly, even while realizing that hundreds of soldiers and innocent people will die or be injured as a result. So we ask for comfort for the families of victims and the release from terrible fear of all affected by the conflict. May war sober us up in realizing that conflict is the result of prejudice and selfishness and vanity that resides in each of us, so may your Spirit heal us. Help us pattern our lives after Jesus, your Son, and to treat other people as He did: where there is suffering, help us bring relief, where there is hatred, help us bring love, where there is guilt and anguish, help us bring forgiveness and healing, where there is fear, help us bring courage and hope.

We pray also for those who bear the Cross of Christ from day to day, those who give of themselves without regard to the cost – for parents who care so deeply that they forget themselves for the sake of their children; for those of faith who sacrifice their time, their energy, and often their very lives, so that those around them who are in need may be satisfied; for those who take the Good News seriously and do all they can to help others to come to know the Saviour. And help each of us to demonstrate our commitment to you by dying to self and coming fully alive to you, so that you may use us and our gifts for the spiritual growth of others. We ask this and all that we pray for, in the name of Jesus, our Saviour and Lord.

AUGUST 23

Almighty God, Creator of all the peoples of the earth, hear our prayers, we ask, for those your children who are in terrible circumstances of conflict or of poverty or of storm. In countries where one political faction fights another, we ask that patience and negotiation will replace hatred and conflict. In the slums of our cities, may those caught in the cycle of poverty be assured of enough to eat, of adequate shelter and of fair opportunities. In areas of the world affected by wind and water and earthquake, give protection, we pray, to those suddenly hit by disasters beyond their control. And provide through the generosity of your people, resources and encouragement to those involved in creating peace, in reducing poverty and in disaster relief. May we all look to the Lord for guidance and hope in a world crying out for peace and calmness.

Your earth, O Lord, also cries out in distress because of polluted waters and contaminated soils, of depleted ozone and a dwindled fishery, of smoggy skies and clear-cut rainforests. Help us who are causing this defilement of your earth to curb our excesses and be more mindful of preserving habitats and creatures, so that your garden can be as Eden again.

O God of the Universe, teach us to have a higher view – to have your perspective – of what a harmonious and tranquil world can be if your people turn to Jesus Christ in faith. Give us enthusiasm for helping others to know Him, so that all men and women will dwell in the fellowship of that Prince of Peace, who lives and reigns with You in the unity of the Holy Spirit, now and forever. Amen.

Lord of all the Universe, it is in awe and wonder that we come to you in worship, with appreciation for the ways in which you have revealed yourself to us not only as Creator, but through Jesus Christ as our Redeemer and Friend. We acknowledge our need of a Redeemer, because we have broken your commands, given in to the battle against evil, uttered words of hurtfulness, withheld your love from others. Forgive us, we pray, in the Name of Jesus, renew us through your Spirit, and enable us to be worthy of your trust in us – to be your faithful servants.

Lord of all seasons, of nature and of experience, we come to you now in gratitude for the past couple of months when many of us have been able to slacken the normal hectic pace in order to spend time with family and to travel and read and relax, and to enjoy the beauty and bounty of the summer. As we gear up for a busy fall season, may we be renewed in energy and in spirit to do those things that match your will for our lives, with a sense of purpose and commitment.

We pray, O Lord, for all who have been affected by accidents and illness over the summer, whether when traveling on the highways, or mishaps at home, or the sudden onslaught of disease – that you would bring solace to those who lost family members and healing to those injured. We ask for your Spirit to also be with all those who have undergone operations or therapy, and with those who are anxious about upcoming medical procedures – that they may know your peace.

We appeal to you, too, in the Name of Jesus the Prince of Peace, asking that your Spirit would influence the minds and consciences of rulers and politicians throughout the world that ways may be found to resolve disputes and prevent combat in countries such as Iraq and Afghanistan and Lebanon and Israel, so that people do not have their lives torn apart or destroyed, but rather live in the absence of war.

We bring to you those who are in positions of authority, whether in government or business, in law enforcement or the courts, in education or the media. Give them wisdom in decision making, compassion in action, vision in planning, and an awareness of your leading in their public and private lives.

O Lord, we ask that you would extend our own vision, our clearness of sight, of what we can accomplish under your direction and coaching; to comprehend your grace, your goodness, your glory; to see that you indeed live within us, prompting us to be more loving, more forgiving, more thoughtful, more peaceful – that we may bring honour to you through our service of Jesus your Son, in whose Name we pray. Amen.

AUTUMN

With praise on our lips we come before you now, Lord of All, thanking you for the promise of your presence and the assurance of your love. To you we owe the best that we have to offer and complete devotion; and yet we confess that we withhold too much of ourselves, fail the tests of temptation, and break your moral commands. So we are grateful, O Lord, that you have redeemed us through Jesus your Son. We echo the Psalmist who said, "Happy are those whose transgression is forgiven, whose sin is covered (Ps. 32:1)."

We are thankful that we can come to you as the Healer of body, mind and spirit, asking for your soothing presence to be with those suffering from disease and accident, from anxiety and depression, from loneliness and lack of hope. May faith in your constant presence give them renewal of hope and peace of mind.

Along with the people of the United States we are reeling from the horror and grief of what happened to their communities this week, with the loss of hundreds of lives and thousands of homes and businesses because of wind and flood and destruction. As rescue and aid reach them, help them to eventually pull together as communities again and to give support to one another and neighbours. We thank you that you have instilled within the human spirit the ability to recover from disaster, and the desire to bolster each other in time of need, and the energy to rebuild lives and homes. As we pause now for a moment of silence, may they be aware of our prayers combined with those of millions of others for them this morning.

As we come to the end of the vacation season, O Lord, we thank you for reminders of how you help us all build community:

- that community is built through institutions of learning – may teachers and professors instill within their students, as they return this week to schools and colleges and universities, a thirst for learning that will motivate them throughout the year
- that community is built through honest business and labour activities – may all who are involved in the workforce find satisfaction in the use of their talents and abilities
- that community is built through institutions of justice – may law enforcement officers and judges act wisely in upholding the laws of our country
- that community is built through good government – may politicians and government workers act with wisdom and integrity in all decision making;
- and that community is built through institutions of faith – help us as a church to worship you with enthusiasm and serve you with faithfulness as we begin a new season of activity.

We thank you, O Lord, that we have the very best news there is for a city and a world in desperate need of hope – that you the Lord of Creation have come to us in human form to bless us and guide us – and this we know through our relationship with Jesus your Son, in whose Name we offer this prayer. Amen.

In the name of Jesus your Son, O God, we extol your majesty, your glory and your creative power. You set the earth on its foundations and filled it with wonderful creatures. Your might is beyond our comprehension. You alone know the secrets of the universe, and your purposes in the world are merely glimpsed by us. Yet you have come among us through your Son, Jesus Christ, who came as a servant of all and gave of Himself for the release of all who are held hostage to sin and death. When tyrants rose against Him, He drank the cup of suffering and was hung on the cross of death, but you raised Him to new life and designated Him a high priest forever, making Him the source of eternal salvation for us and for all who respond to your gracious call.

So we come to you in the Name of Jesus the Redeemer, confessing our need for constant spiritual renewal. Save us, O God, from our aimless wandering, from our idols, from our self-induced chaos. Forgive us for the ways in which we bury your light underneath layers of busyness and denial, and for choosing familiarity, ease, and comfort rather than taking advantage of the opportunities you provide for us in serving others.

We come to you in the Name of Jesus the Advocate, on behalf of those who are disadvantaged – the homeless, the prisoner, the mentally and physically challenged, the persecuted and the poor. May they feel your grace and support through the ways in which we empathize and assist and advocate for them. We come to you in the Name of Jesus the Healer, on behalf of those who are feeling the effects of disease and pain, whether at home or in hospital. May they sense your soothing touch through the skill and care of health professionals and the visits and love of family and friends. Be with those, we pray, affected by hurricane and flood, that they may rebuild their homes and lives with a sense of hope, and with the assistance of all who have traveled to lend a helping hand.

We come to you in the Name of Jesus the Peacemaker, on behalf of those caught up in war and civil strife and terrorist bombings. May they experience your hope through the ways in which we strive for peace in our world. We ask for your presence to continue with family and friends of people who were lost in the tragic events of 9/11, 2001 in the U.S. In the Name of Jesus the Comforter, and on behalf of all those who are experiencing loss, as individuals or on a massive scale, we ask that they may they feel your comfort through our words of sympathy and consolation.

We come to you in the Name of Jesus the Saviour of the world, praying for all who do not yet know His forgiving love. May they come to experience the joy of knowing Him as Friend through the ways in which we are their faith companions and living witnesses to His grace, for all of this we pray for Jesus' sake, and for your glory.

Almighty God, Creator of all that is good and lovely and bountiful, we come to you in worship with gratitude on this beautiful September morning, asking that you would open our eyes to the beauty of the landscape, and the bounty of the fields and gardens, with appreciation for all of the ways in which you nourish and sustain us. We tend to think of ourselves as self-made people, when in fact we are wholly dependent upon the wonder and miracle of the life that you alone have brought into being. So, Author of life, write upon our minds now, we pray, the words that will help us express the deep longings of our hearts for what is true and just and loving as we pray for ourselves, for others, for the world, and for your church.

We pray for ourselves because we need to be delivered from pride and selfishness and envy – all of the things that separate us from the full expression of faithful living. We thank you that deliverance is possible because of our faith in Jesus, your Son, who gave of Himself on the Cross that we might experience forgiveness and be set free to serve you faithfully through the gifts and abilities you have instilled within us. Help us to use all our resources – material and spiritual – with wisdom and with generosity, as you have taught us through your Word.

We pray for others because we are aware of the pain and the worry of illness, and of the hurt and loneliness of grief. For the sick, we ask for your healing touch; for the lonely, your companionship; for the weak, your strength; for the bereaved, your comfort; for the depressed, your love; for the displaced your security. Help us, O God, to see others as though they were Jesus, and thus to give them the full measure of our compassion and devotion.

We pray for our world, which is polluted because of our wastefulness, torn apart because of our wars, depleted because of our consumer mentality. Help us to listen, we pray, to those who show us how to conserve, to those who negotiate peace, and to those who would teach us to be less extravagant. Even as we are enjoying the fruits of the trees and gardens in this fall season, help us, O Lord, to do all we can to preserve and protect your bountiful earth.

We pray, O God, for your Church. We are so privileged to be part of what your Word calls the Body of Christ in the world, and yet are aware of the attacks from without and the diseases within that threaten the health of that Body. Be with those who are suffering persecution because of their faith, with our partners in mission, particularly in Kenya. Be with pastors and lay-people endeavoring to live the Gospel with courage and faithfulness in a secular world. Protect your church, we pray, from division, from moral laxness, and from indifference, that we your people may be wholly devoted to helping others to come fully alive through faith in Jesus Christ, our Lord and Saviour, in whose Name we pray. Amen.

We lift up our voices to you, O Lord, "the everlasting God, the Creator of the ends of the earth (Is. 40:28)," in adoration and praise for the ways in which you have first spoken to us – through the beauty of your Creation, through the revelation of your Word, through the inspiration of your Spirit, through the wisdom of your faithful servants. We are amazed that the One who is responsible for the governing of the whole Universe, is able to call each of us by name, that you love us and discipline us and guide us and forgive us. We acknowledge our need of forgiveness for our rebellion against you, for the breaking of your commandments and for the hurts we have inflicted on others. Through Jesus, who paid the penalty for us, we ask for your forgiving grace.

When we are loaded down with responsibilities and feel powerless and weak, we come to you for the renewal of strength and for a new sense of vision that will allow us to "mount up with wings like eagles" and soar above those things that would restrict our freedom to serve you through the capabilities your Spirit has ingrained within us.

We ask that you would even extend our vision – our clearness of sight – and open our eyes to see beyond the obvious. Help us not to be blind to the deeper needs of those with a hat in hand in the street, or those with a tear on the cheek in the hospital lobby, or those with an out-of-control child in the grocery store, or those caught in a traffic jam on the way to an appointment. Enable us not only to be patient with those we encounter each day, but to be as Christ, offering an encouraging smile, a healing touch, a word of comfort, a gesture of support. We pray also, O Lord, for those who are suffering from accident or disease or virus or mental disorder. Be with those in the midst of or awaiting surgery, or chemotherapy or physiotherapy or counseling and give them freedom from fear, the support of family, and your soothing Spirit. May they feel your healing touch. We pray for the bereaved and ask that you would allow all who are in the midst of grief to experience your enfolding arms of comfort. May faith in you give those who are in distress your strength and peace.

Bring hope for peace to your world, O Lord. Help those affected by bombings in Iraq and Afghanistan and other places in the world not to give in to despair, but to encourage their leaders to negotiate the end of hostilities and work towards lasting reconciliation.

We thank you, O God, for missionaries at home and abroad who make known your reconciling love to those who do not know Jesus as the Lord of their lives. May they have the physical and spiritual stamina for the exhausting work they do, bolstered by the joy of serving you.

Thank you for the privilege we all have of being witnesses to Christ in everyday circumstances. Empower us to be bold yet sensitive, focused yet open, moral yet loving as we seek to honour you, for we ask these things through the Name of Jesus Christ, our Lord and Saviour.

OCTOBER 4

Almighty God, Creator of all that exists, Father of our Lord Jesus Christ, Spirit of Love, we humbly come before you in prayer and praise, feeling deep within our souls gratitude for your listening ear and merciful grace. We thank you for the beauty and the gifts of this autumn season: the bountiful fields and gardens, the crimson and yellow trees, the cool relief from summer heat. May the abundance of food remind us to share it with the hungry; may the colour prompt us to refrain from graying your world with pollution; may the chill in the air remind us not to be cold toward others. We need these reminders because we have short memories that need your Word for inspiration and guidance in how we live and how we treat others and how we respect your world. Your Word also tells us of the way in which Jesus lived, offering healing and hope and forgiveness; encouraging us to love one another as He has loved us.

We thank you, O Lord, for the ways in which you have prompted this congregation to demonstrate care and concern for the people of this city, and give you gratitude for the work of volunteers of organizations such as Out of the Cold, and House of Compassion, and Habitat for Humanity, and Meals on Wheels, and Churches on the Hill Food Bank, and various shelters for the refugee, the homeless and the youth, and the Good Works support group for the unemployed. Give them the energy and resources they need to be as Christ to others.

We thank you for the freedoms we experience in this country and province and city, and for the right to vote. We ask that your Spirit would give guidance and wisdom to those who govern and administer, and ask your blessing particularly upon the federal parliament as the Members of Parliament resume the business of governing our country this week.

We thank you for Jesus the Great Physician, asking for His healing strength to be with those who are ill at home or in hospital; and that their families too will feel the gentle touch of your Spirit upon them in times of worry and stress.

We are grateful, O Lord, that Jesus also gave of Himself for us on the Cross, thereby taking our guilt upon Himself and freeing us from its eternal consequences. As we later participate in the Lord's Supper may we not only be spiritually refreshed but also reminded of our own responsibility to put behind us all grudges and to be merciful to others.

All of these things we ask in the Name of Jesus, to whom we humbly bow and eagerly confess that He is the Lord of our lives and the Saviour of the world; and to you be all glory and honour and praise.

Along with the Psalmist (145), we extol you, our God and King, and bless your name forever and ever. On the glorious splendor of your majesty, we will meditate; and the might of your awesome deeds we shall proclaim in our prayer.

On this weekend set aside by our whole culture to offer thanks, we bow ourselves before you now, O God, in humble acknowledgment that all of the gratitude expressed this day needs to be directed to you the Lord of Creation. Even as the bounty of your earth is displayed before us, we offer thanks for the wonderful tastes and smells and sights of this harvest season, for the colourful landscapes of the countryside, for the reunion of families around dinner tables, and for the privilege of generously sharing our abundance with those in need.

We do admit, however, that we are not as generous as you, Lord. We do things for others with mixed motives, we withhold mercy when it is most needed, we fall into selfishness, moral laxness and envy, and we fail to live up to our full potential as your children. We need your grace and mercy, so above all on this Thanksgiving Sunday, we express our gratitude for your generous love, offered to us without condition, exemplified most amazingly through forgiveness, and demonstrated through the sacrifice of Jesus Christ on our behalf.

We pray in Jesus' Name for people in need of healing, and relief from pain and disease, and protection from fear and despair. Through the skill of doctors and surgeons, the care of nurses and therapists, the love of family and friends, and the hope of your Spirit, may they find healing and comfort and peace.

We pray in Jesus' Name for political and community leaders

who need your guidance, for social workers and service agencies who need your counsel, for police and fire fighters and soldiers and peacemakers who need your protection, and for religious leaders and charities who need your direction.

We pray in Jesus' Name for children and youth: that they may garner wisdom as well as knowledge in school, and benefit from exercise as well as fun on the sports field, and find guidance as well as nurturing from parents and teachers. Protect them, we pray, from the pressures and temptations of our fast-paced society, and draw them closer to yourself in faith.

We pray also that you would help us all to be peacemakers in your world, to emphasize negotiation rather than confrontation, to respect and protect our environment, and to demonstrate tolerance toward all the cultures of our community, in order that the influence of your Spirit may be felt in all that we do and say for your praise and glory, and in the Name of Jesus Christ, with thanksgiving.

We come to you, Lord, the One who is our Maker and our Sustainer, to offer a prayer of gratitude and praise from the depths of our souls. We thank you that your power extends beyond our strengths and achievements, that the towers we build and the rockets we launch never begin to touch the vastness of your heaven, that you are always more than we can imagine or proclaim. We offer our gratitude for all your gifts to us – for daily food – for healing and health – for each breath we take – for freedom to choose – and for the gifts of your Word, your guidance, and your love. Our minds are truly overwhelmed, O God, when we consider all that you are and how you have entrusted so much to us. May we be worthy of that trust – may we be a people who are unafraid to live as fully and as richly as you want us to live.

We thank you, Lord, that the mysteries of your Creation keep us from the foolishness of worshiping the works of our own hands, though in weak moments we still bow to the idols of materialism. In fact, O Lord, we have too many weak moments. We give in too easily to the temptations that plague us, sinning against you and hurting those around us. Forgive us, we pray, for those thoughts and actions that separate us from you: our pride and jealousy, our anger and grudges, selfishness and greed, our indifference and prejudices. We appeal to you in the name of Jesus to forgive us, to set us free from the guilt, and to give us the strength to resist further temptation. Help us O God, to be faithful followers of Jesus, to multiply all that you give us, to spread your Word even at the risk of seeing it misunderstood, to dare to love those whom others think worthy only of hate, to take chances by doing good to those who have not done good to us. Make us people who share in both word and action that which you have given to us to do.

We pray, too, for those who are poor in body or in spirit; for those who are oppressed and persecuted for their faith; for those who are sick or in grief or despair. Minister, O Lord, by your Spirit, and through us, to all those who need your Word of healing and comfort and hope.

We pray for you Church in the world, O God. Give your guidance to missionaries and staff of Canadian Baptist Ministries, that they will continue to faithfully proclaim the Good News in this country and in the broader world to those who have never known Jesus. Give them continued courage and stamina that their witness will not be in vain and that others may see that they have the greatest news in the world to share.

Help us in this congregation to also see as our chief priority the proclamation of Jesus Christ as the Saviour and Friend of all in this our own city and mission field, for we ask these things in His Name.

Almighty God, it is with gratitude that we come to you in prayer, for you are our Creator, our Provider, and our Redeemer. We bow our heads in humility, knowing that in ourselves there is no worthiness; but we come also in confidence, knowing that Jesus has made us worthy through His death on the Cross. We acknowledge that like the disciples, we are slow at understanding who Jesus is, too quick to abandon Him when faced with danger or ridicule, too easily swayed by the allure of power or money. Our sins are many, and have caused a rift in our relationship with you. So we humbly ask for your forgiveness in the Name of Jesus, and that we will have the soundness of character to forgive others. Teach us how to forgive those who have injured us, gossiped against us, and treated us unjustly or indifferently. Help us to be in control of our desires, restrain us from selfishness, keep us from wanting what others have, prevent us from growing hard and cruel and cynical, enable us to cultivate the spirit of a hope which never dies and of a love that never fails.

Lord God, help us to be kind to one another, to sacrifice our own comforts for the sake of others, to care for those who suffer, to have a heart of compassion, to have a tongue that utters words of mercy, and hands that perform works of healing. Assist us, O God, to be more expressive in our relationship with you – to show forth your boundless generosity through our own caring. Grant us, O Lord, courage in our obedience to you and strength in our service.

We bring to your seat of mercy those affected by the wars that nations inflict upon one another. As guns rattle and bombs explode, help us to be incensed enough by the injuries and death of innocent people that we will write to political leaders, cry out for justice, and demonstrate peace by the way we live. When we see people traumatized by hatred and bigotry, help us to personally fight prejudice, not only from afar, but within our communities and within our own hearts.

We pray also, O Lord, for the victims of hurricane and flood and starvation. Help us, through organizations such as Sharing Way, to be generous in providing money and resources for the people affected by these devastating natural disasters. May those distributing food and materials on site have the physical and emotional energy to deal with the chaos and relieve the suffering of the many thousands in need.

We thank you, O God, for the community of your Church, where we freely worship and serve you, where we gather for encouragement and for companionship, where we combine our resources for the betterment of others, and where we patiently wait for the full unveiling of your Kingdom through the return of our Lord Jesus Christ, in whose name we pray.

NOVEMBER 1

With awe and wonder and gratitude we come to you in prayer, O God, thanking you that we are able to enjoy all of the senses you instill within us. We recognize the beauty of autumn colour only because you give us sight; we harken to the inspiration of a hymn because you give us hearing; we respond to the touch of a friend because you give us feeling; we enjoy bread and meat because you give us taste; we sniff the aromas of nature because you give us the sense of smell. From you, O Lord, come also emotion and hope and initiative. Instill within us now, we pray, not only appreciation for all of these benefits of body and mind, but also for faith, and for the forgiving love that we have experienced through knowing your Son, Jesus Christ.

We confess with sorrow that we use our senses for sin as well as benefit, and give in to passions that lead us away, rather than draw us closer, to you. Forgive us, we pray, release us from guilt, renew us in spirit, that we may be freed up to serve you through the gifts and abilities imparted to us through your Spirit.

You also make us conscious of the needs of others. As we pause now in a moment of silence, we bring to you family members and friends who are ill, in need of your compassionate touch....

And for those who are in grief, in need of your comfort....

And for those who could use a friend, in need of your companionship....

We pray too for the children and teens of our congregation. Protect them from accident and abuse, from peer pressure, from the lure of materialism; and give them wisdom as well as knowledge, and the assurance of family support, and the stability of faith. May they take on as a Friend for life, Jesus our Saviour.

And now, O Lord, we ask that you would make each of us a missionary of the Gospel in our own life-settings. Help us to run with determination the race that is set before us that we may be your faithful and energetic people in this mission field of Toronto, for we ask this in the Name of Jesus your Son.

Remembrance Day

Almighty and everlasting God, Lord of mercy and of love, we approach you now in humility, conscious of the sacrifice that you made on our behalf through the death of our Lord Jesus Christ on the Cross. On this day we remember, also, others who paid the ultimate sacrifice to defend our freedom and peace, and humbly reflect on the ways our lives have been changed or enhanced by the thousands of men and women who gave of themselves for us in times of war. Forgive us, O God, for not remembering them fittingly, by forgetting, through our own neglect of striving for peace, why they sacrificed their lives.

Lord of Light, source of all that is eternal – be with us through the dark hours of unease and worry, especially when it seems that the world around us is falling apart because of terrorist attacks and the threat of war. Help us to remember that you are ultimately in charge of all things and that your Spirit of comfort will be with those who have lost loved ones to war and those who are traumatized by conflict. May their faith in you give them hope, and the desire to triumph over the evil surrounding them.

Gracious and merciful God, we thank you for your unconditional love – a love that accepts us as we are, and embraces us with warmth and encouragement when we stumble and fall, and a love which forgives us when we rebel against you and hurt others. Help us O God to be faithful in extending that same love to all around us.

O God of peace and reconciliation, we ask for your presence and protection with our Canadian Peacekeeping Forces in Afghanistan and other areas of unrest in the world. Give them wisdom in making quick-thinking decisions in conflict, and patience in the midst of negotiation, and hope for the peaceful resolution of hostilities. May their families know your peace, even in their times of loneliness and worry.

We pray also for those who maintain public peace here at home, particularly our police and security forces. Give them protection while on duty, whether in combatting crime or dealing with domestic disputes or confronting gang warfare or dealing with traffic offences; and enable us as citizens to give them the respect they are due.

O God of mercy and compassion, of comfort and of healing, may the tender touch of your Spirit be upon those in hospital and home who live in illness and fear and despair. We pray that you would bless them with your healing Spirit in the midst of their discomfort and loneliness and struggle. Be also with those who are mourning the loss of relatives and friends, that they may know the consolation of eternal hope.

We ask for your comfort to be with the survivors of earthquake and flood in Pakistan and Kashmir, that relief efforts will be able to reach those in remote villages before the heavy onset of winter, and that those offering aid will have the energy and endurance and resources necessary for giving help to people in desperate circumstances.

We ask these things in Jesus' Name.

NOVEMBER 15

O Lord of earth and sky and sea and life, of beauty and love and joy and hope, we come to you now in prayer, full of confidence that you will continue to meet all our needs, physical and emotional and social and spiritual, because we know you as our Holy Parent and the Lord of our lives. We are grateful to you, O God, for creating us, nourishing us, teaching us and encouraging us, unworthy though we are. We confess that we are often selfish and uncaring, angry and vengeful, boastful and proud for the wrong reasons, so we come to you also asking for the pardoning of sin, for forgiveness in the Name of Jesus your Son, the One who died on the Cross to free us from guilt and to give us new and eternal life.

We pray, O Lord, for the health of your people and of your world. May your healing strength be with those in beds of sickness at home or hospital; may your encouraging Spirit be with those feeling the November Blues in these days of decreasing sunlight and drab landscape; may your comforting love be with those experiencing the emptiness of grief and the sorrow of loss, that all might experience the hope of faith. And for your suffering world, whose resources we continue to deplete and whose firmament we pollute, we ask for your intervention in changing our consumer attitudes and practices that we might be more responsible stewards of your earth and sky and sea, and of all that lives.

We pray, too, for your suffering people, O Lord – those affected by the cruelty of others, victims of crime and war and prejudice. Help us not to add to their distress through uncaring attitudes but as followers of Jesus to treat people in the same way He did, with acceptance and compassion, with honesty and

111

forgiveness.

We pray for Christ's Church in the world, O God, and for our own Baptist Convention of Ontario and Quebec, that wise decisions may be made in the midst of difficult social and theological issues, so that, above all, Jesus is glorified and His mission advanced. Also, give your guidance to missionaries and staff of Canadian Baptist Ministries, that they will continue to faithfully proclaim the Good News in this country and in the broader world to those who have never known Jesus. We ask, too, that you would be with your followers who are persecuted for their faith. Give them continued courage and stamina that their witness will not be in vain and that others may see that they have the greatest news in the world to share.

Help us in this congregation to also see as our chief priority the proclamation of Jesus Christ as the Saviour and Friend of all in this our own city and mission, for we ask these things in His Name.

Eternal God, Lord of all we experience, we call upon you now in prayer in order to be refreshed in mind and spirit. Speaking to you not only renews us but gives us a perspective on life that encourages hope rather than despair, and trust rather than fear. We thank you for the signs of promise you provide through the Scriptures. Through Noah you gave us the rainbow as a sign that you would give us eternal protection, through Moses you gave us the law tablets as the sign of your moral guidance, and through Jesus you gave us the Cross as a sign of your everlasting mercy and grace – a mercy and grace that opens up for us the gates of your Kingdom. In these signs we recognize and acknowledge your love which sustains us and motivates us each day.

We thank you that it is also a forgiving love, for we confess to you in sorrow that we too often ignore your presence in our lives, giving in to temptations and passions that lead us away from you. When the battle of good and evil rages within and around us, and our ancient foe tempts us with his deceits and empty promises, we ask that you would keep us faithful to your Word and, when we fall, raise us again and restore us through your Son, Christ Jesus, in whose name we ask for your forgiveness.

We ask that you would bless those who are suffering today – particularly those in hospital and nursing homes, and give them relief through the help of doctors, nurses and caregivers, and an awareness of the prayers and support of family and friends.

Be with those who grieve, we pray, and let them know the solace and the promise of eternal hope. Lift them from despair and grant to them the assurance of your comforting and saving love.

On these cold winter days and nights, we think of those who have to work outdoors, and ask that you would keep them safe as they labor to keep the rest of us in comfort. Be with the homeless and hungry, as well as with those who provide shelter and food for them.

We pray, too, O Lord, for those who are caught up in war, the innocent people who are affected by bombs and embargoes and land mines, that you would give them your protection. Help the leaders of the nations to make decisions that will lead to peace rather than hostility, and inspire us all to be peacemakers through the way in which we treat one another.

Again we thank you, O God, that we know you through Jesus, who became one of us, identifies and empathizes with us, and encourages us through the power of the Spirit to bring the wonderful good news of your offer of salvation to all around us, for we ask these things in His Name.

NOVEMBER 29

O God of all creation, we come to you who, in the beginning, created light and all that illumines our world and thank you for the myriad ways in which you bring brightness into our lives. As we begin the Advent Season by lighting a candle of hope, we thank you that our hope rests in you rather than in ourselves or in any misconceptions of what we can accomplish without your grace and guidance. We acknowledge with sadness that we cave in to temptations and selfish desires that result in despair rather than hope, in turmoil rather than peace, in misery rather than joy and in prejudice rather than love. Forgive us our sins, we pray, and remake us in the image of Jesus, who brings hope and wholeness to all who come to you in His Name.

It is in Jesus that we find strength for each day, no matter what may be afflicting us, so we pray now for those who are ill, whether in hospital or at home; for those facing treatments, whether chemo or physio; for those who are depressed, whether in mind or in spirit, that your spirit of hope would encourage and heal them. We pray also for those who are hungry or home-less, prejudiced against or persecuted; lonely or isolated, that they may discover a caring community of your people, even us, willing to offer hope and shelter and companionship.

We pray, O Lord, for this your church, and ask for your blessing upon all of its ministries and programs and mission endeavors. Be with the Deacons as they meet this week that they may give wise vision and compassionate spiritual care to our congregation. Be with the Board of Mission as they inform us of the work of Canadian Baptist Ministries and Sharing Way and foster our support of mission endeavors in our own city. Be with all involved in our Christian Education program, that through the Sunday School and Bible Studies and Alpha and Youth ministries we may be informed People of the Book. Be with the Board of Finance and Administration as they encourage us to be generous in all aspects of Christian stewardship. Be with the Board of Music and Choir, that they will continue to inspire us through the music of this Advent Season. Be with the Trustees as they both protect and use the assets and trust funds and properties of the congregation for the financial stability of our ministries. Be with the Yorkminster Park Women, as they foster fellowship and nourishment and mission education in our life as the Body of Christ. And be with all our ministry and support staff as we gear up for this busy Advent Season, that we may not lose sight of our reason to be a church – to bring to those of our community the good news of Jesus' coming into our world, and of the marvelous impact He has had on all of our lives, for these things we ask in His Name.

WINTER

DECEMBER 6

Almighty God, Creator and Enabler of all, on this Sunday of Advent Hope we come to you in prayer with thanksgiving and gladness in our hearts for the promise of your coming into our lives, and the return of Jesus to our earth. As a candle has been brought to flame this morning, so bring us to shine as candles of hope in this world of darkness and despair.

We come to you with sadness in our hearts because so many people live seemingly without hope because of poverty or abuse or illness or sorrow. We ask for your compassionate care with those who suffer hardship and the breakdown of hope among us. We pray for older people whose pension cheques cannot stretch far enough. For single parents who are forced to choose between paying rent and buying food. For men and women who find themselves without work. For employers who barely make the payroll from month to month, and employees who try to hide their fear of getting laid off. For families forced to abandon their homes for a new community where no one knows their names. For all others whose circumstances we do not know, but who need a special blessing at this time, we ask that you would challenge us to be more understanding, and to help where we can.

On this day when we think particularly of those infected with HIV and AIDS virus, we ask that you would be with the 40 million children, women and men suffering from this terrible scourge. Give your guidance, we pray, to the medical and pharmaceutical companies endeavoring to find a preventative cure, and to the doctors and nurses and palliative care workers who are treating and comforting those who are suffering. This, too, we bring to you, the God of Hope.

In a day when the problems that confront us seem more than we can handle, we ask that you would open our eyes to the resources at our command as your children, and make us grateful for them. We thank you for minds that can think, for hearts that can feel, for eyes that give us vision, and for hands that can do. We thank you for large purposes that call us into your service, for causes that unite us, and for your grace that restores and forgives us.

We need your forgiveness, Lord, for we are sinful people. We remember now the temptations we have willfully given in to, the sins we have committed, the harm we have done to other people and to ourselves, and the rift we have caused between us and you.

Yet you have not abandoned us. Rather than giving us up as hopeless, you have continually welcomed us back, as the father did the prodigal, and placed over our shoulders the cloak of forgiveness; and on our feet the sandals of faith, and on our finger the ring of hope, and offered to us the banquet of companionship and love.

And so in faith we come to you the God of Hope. You are the Source of the love which alone can make the hope come alive. We claim that hope through Jesus your Son, through whom your promises come true, and in whose name we pray.

Lord God, beyond our deserving, you invite us into your holy presence, and we are grateful. As we turn to you now in prayer, it is in awe, yet in confidence. In awe of your holiness, your creative power and your justice; in confidence because of your love and patience and mercy. We come humbly, recognizing our need of your forgiveness. Our sinfulness has caused rifts that only you can bridge, and wounds that only the blood of your Son Jesus can heal; so in His Name we plead for your forgiveness and savor your mercy.

We live in a fractured world, O God, and on this day of Advent Peace ask that your Spirit of Peace would influence those who have the power to promote or resist change – the leaders of government and industries, the writers of books and newspapers, the teachers of our schools and universities, and the leaders of our churches. Give them, we pray, a sense of responsibility to hope and work for the best of which they are capable, and use their influence to convince people of the futility of greed and prejudice and hostility.

O God of all, strengthen each of us to live every day on a high level of Christian conduct; inspire us to meet whatever comes with calm courage, resolute purpose and a compassionate spirit. Grant us victory over selfish tendencies, the power to conquer hate, and wisdom to follow your leading.

We pray also for those who bear their own cross from day to day, those who give of themselves without regard to the cost – for parents who care so deeply that they forget themselves for the sake of their children; for those who give up their own plans in order to look after sick or elderly relatives, for those of faith who sacrifice their time, their energy, and often their very lives, so that those around them who are in need may be satisfied; for those who take the Good News seriously and do all they can to help others to come to know the Saviour. And help each of us to demonstrate our commitment to you by dying to self and coming fully alive to you, so that you may use us and our gifts for the spiritual growth of others. Help us to be seeds that bear much fruit.

Give us, we pray, a deep sense of fellowship as we worship here together. Increase our faith in the things that can never die: the dream of peace and security for people everywhere. Keep us working, praying, sacrificing, persevering, for we ask this and all that we pray for, in the name of your Son and our Lord, Jesus.

Along with the angels on high, we glory in the drama of your coming, O Christ. That you should depart the realm of heaven, even for a time, for us, is beyond our understanding. The carols of the season aid us in expressing the wonder of your appearance, but the awesomeness of the motive would remain a mystery to us, were it not through grace and love. Forgiveness, too, which we are greatly in need of. We admit our sins of commission and omission and acknowledge that they have created a great chasm between you and us, a chasm that has only been bridged by your broken body, laid down for us. Thank you for coming to us not only as the Messiah Child, but as the Redeeming Saviour.

We also know you as the Great Physician. Even as you brought healing and comfort and peace of mind to those we read of in the Gospels, so we ask for your grace to be with our family members and friends and congregational companions who are suffering either from illness, or from grief. Give them hope, O Lord, and an awareness of the love and support of others.

We know you, too, O Christ, as the One who fed the five thousand. There are more than that in our city and land who need our contribution to the loaves and fishes miracle. We thank you for inspiring those who contribute and serve through the food banks and Christmas baskets and Out of the Cold programs in order that others may be fed and clothed and sheltered, and ask that you would encourage us all to be more generous.

We come to you also as the Prince of Peace, even as others are engaged in war or planning for it. We know that individuals and nations have a need to defend themselves from aggressors and terrorists, and that there are no simple solutions; but we pray that the divine influences of forgiveness and understanding and compassion might be the determining factors at the bargaining tables and councils, so that people may not have to live in fear.

We thank you again for this Advent Season. Though we feel rushed and stressed at times, we know that our faith in you, the Christ, can calm our souls and slow our feet, at least enough to rejoice in the miracle of your coming and savor the true flavors of the season – the hope and peace and love and joy you instill within us. In your Name we pray.

O Lord God, and Holy Parent of us all, we come to you with gratitude that you have revealed yourself through Jesus our Saviour, born with divine connections but into a human family. We thank you for these Christmas celebrations as we remember His birth and glory in the fact that we can identify with Him who became part of our human family in such a wonderful way. We pray for members of our own families now. For infants and toddlers as they develop motor skills and emotional responses; for children and teens as they discover lessons in the schools of learning and of experience; for young people as they face challenging opportunities and choose careers; for those who are embarking on marriage, and for those who are having difficulties in their marriage; for parents as they offer moral and spiritual guidance to their daughters and sons; and for grandparents and aunts and uncles who provide continuing stability and wise counsel to their families.

May your reconciling Spirit transform family life when it becomes tense or fractured. When we become estranged from relatives because of past disagreements, give us the courage to take the first step toward reconciliation, to write a letter or make a phone call or pay a visit; and to depend upon your Spirit to change hearts and attitudes. We ask that you would help all of us to work at strengthening our family life and to model our behaviour on instructions from your Word.

The Church is your family, O Lord, and we ask that you would uphold all members of this family of Yorkminster Park Baptist Church, whether we are single or married; whether we have lost a spouse through death or through divorce; whether we are young or middle aged or elderly, and inspire us to be not simply tolerant of one another, but loving and compassionate and supportive.

And finally, O Lord, we ask that you would give us a deep longing to invite others to be part of this your Family – to celebrate not only this Christmas season, but the marvelous ongoing privilege of caring for all who would be your children, for we ask these things in the name of Jesus our Lord.

We come to you this night with an overwhelming feeling of gratitude, O God. That you should visit this small planet in the vastness of the universe, and love us enough to send your Son, is beyond our imagining. How we thank you for your Word in which we read of Jesus' humble birth in Bethlehem, though it was heralded by the Angels of Heaven, and marveled at by the shepherds of the fields, and honoured by the kings of the East, with their gifts.

We thank you for this season of gift-giving, of the exchange of cards and letters, of delicious meals shared with family and friends, of the music of the carols, and of decorations and celebrations. But, above all, we thank you for this time of shared worship when we are reminded of the timeless gift of Jesus the Messiah – the One who has had an enormous impact on our world and our individual lives and our families.

We ask that you would uphold all members of this family of Yorkminster Park Baptist Church and inspire us to be loving and compassionate and supportive of one another in this Christmas season, and throughout the coming year.

As the Christ Candle was lit this evening, we thank you that it was surrounded, as we are, by the promises of hope and peace and joy and love – themes that remind us that our faith is grounded in Jesus Christ, the Light of the World, and which enable us to live in harmony with one another.

It is with gratitude for allowing us the wonderful privilege of being lighted candles in our homes and communities that we pray in the Name of Jesus our Saviour. Amen.

God of the Ages, on this first Sunday of a new year, we praise you whose Realm is everlasting, whose Word is truth and whose Justice is tempered with love. We appreciate the resources of your Creation that nourish and sustain us on a daily basis; and thank you for the shelter and warmth and dignity of this your sanctuary for worship. As we approach you now with reverence, we pray that you will receive us into your enfolding arms of grace.

We thank you that it is a grace that embodies forgiveness, which we need. We confess our sins with sorrow. To you we owe obedience, yet we have rebelled against your laws; to you we owe loyal service, yet we have neglected our responsibilities; from you we have been offered forgiveness, yet we have often refused to forgive others. Have mercy on us, O God, subdue our rebellious spirits, humble our pride, and grant us forgiveness of our sins through Jesus Christ, that we may begin this new year with renewed commitment.

We thank you, O Lord, for your Church universal, and for the opportunity we have of serving Jesus through this local congregation. May your Church continue to be a fountain of truth in this city and in the world, and a channel through which your love reaches all people. Bless our Queen and those who govern our country, O God. We pray that power may not corrupt those who hold public office, but prompt them always to use their authority to check what is evil and to encourage all that is good. We praise you for all your servants who have done justice, loved mercy and walked humbly with you. We praise you, O God, for all those who have answered your call to preach the Good News of the Gospel, and for those who have devoted their lives to sharing the inspiration of the Holy Scriptures with others, whether it be at home or in other lands. We praise you, O God, for those who show compassion to the poor, feed the hungry and shelter the homeless; for those who work towards peace in a warring world; and for those who welcome the stranger and offer mercy and forgiveness to those who have strayed from your path. We praise you, O God, for those who are willing to lose their own independence in service to others, caring for the sick, comforting the dying, visiting the lonely, consoling those in grief. We ask for your compassionate and healing touch to be with the sick and your comforting peace to be with them.

We also honor the memory of those individuals of this congregation who have lived among us and shared their faith in personal ways, who have finished the race and now inhabit the heavenly realm with you. Help us to honour their memory by the way in which we live and love. Continue to be with us in this service of worship and through Communion, we pray, that we may glory in your presence and further commit ourselves to faithfully serve our Lord and Saviour, Jesus Christ, in whose name we ask all these things.

Creator God, Lord of the whole Universe, yet Holy Parent to each of your children, we worship you in thankfulness and humility, affirming you as the One who made all things through the motivation of love. Your mercy and your compassion have no limits. Your grace and your forgiveness are greater than we can express in words alone, and so we come to you with humble hearts, expressing our gratitude that we know you through Jesus Christ, who has established a new covenant with us, and has imprinted the law of love and forgiveness on our hearts. We are rebellious and sinful, so we thank you that participation in your family, the Church, gives us the remedy of dealing with a guilty conscience—that through Jesus' love we are able to begin each day fresh and renewed.

We pray for a sense of renewal in the lives of others, O God; for those afflicted with injury from accident, and those fighting disease and illness, and those who have been traumatized by murder and crime, and those who need relief from all the stress in their lives. We pray for the healing power of your Spirit to be with those who are ill. We thank thee that we can know peace, in spite of the turmoil about us, because of the assurance that you are always beside us and within us and ahead of us as the Lord of our lives.

We thank you that we know you, the One who brought form and substance out of the chaos, and continues to give us hope and joy and beauty and companionship. We thank you for Jesus, Our Friend, and ask you now to help us pattern our lives after Him, and to treat other people as Jesus did: where there is illness and suffering, help us bring caring relief; where there is hatred, help us bring reconciling love; where there is guilt, help us bring healing forgiveness; and where there is fear, help us bring hopeful courage.

Give us also a heart, O God, for those who do not know Jesus, the Wonderful Saviour, and enable us to overcome the reluctance to tell our own story of how He has changed our lives.

We thank you, O Lord, for those who are offering themselves to you through the waters of baptism this morning. May their example inspire us all to be living witnesses, determined to leave this house of worship confident that your Spirit will provide us with the energy and passion to live in faithful service of our Lord and Saviour Jesus Christ, in whose Name we pray.

It is with awesome wonder that we approach you now, Creator and Lord of all, full of amazement that you should listen and respond to us. Your love enriches our lives, your mercy humbles us and your forgiveness astounds us.

On this day in which we pray for Christian unity, we thank you for the witness in this community of each of the Churches On The Hill, and for the ways in which they work cooperatively through discussion and worship to proclaim the Good News of Jesus to our neighbours. Be with all ministers, as they bring the truth of your Word to our ears this morning. We pray for your Church universal: for individual Christians who are faithful and loving; for denominational leaders who are visionary and sound in Christian character; for missionaries at home and abroad who lead others to you. Help us to be faithful to the words of Jesus who prayed that we might be one in our devotion to Him. Draw us closer to you and to our brothers and sisters in Christ Jesus that we may better know your will and work cooperatively together that others might experience the fullness of your grace. Help us to be faithful to your call to us to be fishers of men and women – to be your ambassadors and your ministers of reconciliation in the world.

Help us also, O Lord, to work together for issues of justice and peace when we see the world in its darkness. Help us to know what to do, what to say, and how to say it, so the leaders of the nations will hear and respond. When we see abuses of power and wealth, help us to be examples of humility and generosity. When we see epidemic diseases help us to be healing agents. When we see poverty, help us to enrich others. Enable us, we pray, to reflect the life of Jesus in the ways in which we promote peace and help the people of the world to know that nothing can ever separate us from your love.

All of these things we pray for in His Name, and for the sake of your Church.

We come to you on this winter Sunday morning, O God, feeling the bite of cold on the outside but the warmth of Christian fellowship on the inside, knowing that you are the One who provides sanctuary from cold weather – and cold hearts – and enhances our lives with a consoling faith and rich companionship. Yet we acknowledge that we are often unappreciative of your protection from the evil things that threaten and are vulnerable to the world's temptations and influence, and give in to sin too easily. Help us to accept the freedom of your forgiveness and the light of your guidance. We thank you that through Jesus Christ we have been delivered from guilt and are now able to use the spiritual gifts you have instilled within us to bring others to a saving knowledge of His presence in their lives.

We thank you for your Word, O God, which encouraged us to build protective walls of shelter and support, helping others to feel safe in a threatening world; forgive us when we build walls of exclusion and prejudice that exclude others from the sanctum of faith and fellowship. Help us to be welcoming Christians, treating as guests those who come through the Out of the Cold program, or for food coupons, or for help from the Benevolent Fund. Be with all volunteers of these ministries and of Meals On Wheels, of House of Compassion, of Youth Unlimited, of Matthew House, and of the food banks and shelters for the homeless in this city, and give them your encouraging Spirit.

We pray through Jesus the Great Physician, that you would bring healing and strength and hope to those who are suffering in hospital or at home. May they be supported through the treatment of physicians and nurses and caregivers, and encouraged by relatives and friends.

We come to you the Great Comforter, O God, asking that you would be with the families of civilians and soldiers killed in bombings in Iraq and Afghanistan this week, and of the hundreds in the continuing conflicts in Sudan and Kenya and the Gaza Strip. May your Spirit influence the minds and consciences of rulers and politicians who are planning for war or are in the midst of conflict. May they find ways of resolving disputes and preventing combat so that people will not have their lives torn apart or destroyed, but rather live in the hope of peace.

Enable us who are here this morning to be faithful ambassadors of Jesus Christ, who brings peace of mind to all who come to Him, offering their lives in humble service, for we ask these things in and through the Name of Jesus, our Lord and Saviour.

In awe and wonder and praise we come to you now, O God, expressing gratitude for provision of our needs, for family and friends, for minds to think and plan, for work and leisure, for opportunities of worship and the privilege of prayer; and above all for your love and mercy and forgiveness. We need your forgiveness because we are rebellious in nature, often disobeying your moral commands, and in the process alienating ourselves from you and others. Thank you for coming to us through Jesus, the great Reconciler, who gave of himself on the Cross that we might know release from guilt, and the renewal of relationships, and joy in life.

We acknowledge, however, that there are many people not feeling joyful this morning. We pray for those in pain through chronic illness, whether it be arthritis or headache or cancer or angina or other diseases – give them release from discomfort, and the courage to continue living in hope. May your peace and presence continue with those who are ill. Be with those ministering to them: the doctors, nurses, therapists, family members, friends and pastors – that they may offer compassion and consolation, companionship and loving support.

In your mercy we ask for your presence with those not feeling joyful because they have no bed to call their own, and those struggling to make ends meet for their families, and those who cope with mental illness and depression, and those who are marginalized because of race or religion or economic circumstances. Help us not to contribute to their difficulties by ignoring them or ridiculing them or being prejudiced against them or by feeling superior in any way, but rather make us into the image of Christ who empathized with all and pointed each of us to you.

We pray for those finding it difficult to feel joy because of war and oppression and fear of terrorists. So we ask for the end of hostilities in war-torn countries such as Kenya and Sudan and Iraq and Afghanistan and Gaza, that the people might have political stability and peace in their lands.

We pray for those of our own city fearful of violence and crime, and especially for the families of those recently shot simply for being in the wrong place at the wrong time on the street. May the police and social agencies and churches who are endeavoring to combat unrest in our neighbourhoods be given the resources and support they need from all citizens.

We ask that you would be with those endeavoring to bring food and supplies to the millions in the world suffering from starvation and flooding and storm. May individuals and nations respond with generosity so that others will have relief from hunger.

We pray, O Lord, for ourselves. Not that we might be affluent, but more generous; not that we might be content, but more compassionate; not that we might be self-satisfied, but self-giving. Help us to see that true joy is found in knowing you, and not in being content with present circumstances. And enable us to pass on to others an understanding of that true joy in order that they may come to you, the Giver of life. May your Name be honoured in all that we do, for we ask these things through your Son, Jesus Christ our Lord.

Lord of all, Saviour of all, Friend of all who would come to you in faith, we approach you now in thankfulness that on a February morning we are sheltered and warmed by this place of worship and by your presence. Yet we deserve to shiver in your presence – we who so often choose to be out in the cold of lone-liness and the darkness of sin. That you should constantly choose to welcome us into the enfolding, comforting, forgiving arms of faith is a mystery to us, but we read in your Word of how Jesus did just that: of how he entered the home of a tax collecting cheater, of how he drove a multitude of devils out of a disturbed man, of how he forgave a woman of the streets – all representa-tive of us who have our own secrets and devils and sins to contend with. We thank you, O God, that you see through us and beyond us, that you encourage our potential, that you offer us hope. Yet we know that "Our hope is built on nothing less than Jesus' blood and righteousness;" so it is in His Name on this Communion Sunday that we ask for your forgiveness, and lay ourselves before you for remaking and renewal.

Our world is in need of restructuring too, O Lord. We hear and see and read in the media of how people are trauma-tized by war, victimized by crime, and terrorized by cruelty; and we personally experience lifestyle-induced illnesses, and family arguments and work related stresses. That's why we are so glad to be able to turn to you in the Name of Jesus, the One who empathizes, understands, reconciles, and loves beyond measure.

We appeal to you, Lord, on behalf of those who are ill, whether it is the flu or cancer, a heart condition or an injury, an infection or a mental disorder. May they feel your healing and comforting touch, and know that they are loved and prayed for.

We ask for your healing presence to be with them.

And in a week in which we are feeling keenly the sting of death, we ask for your comforting love to be with the grieving. May they feel our support as a congregation in the days to come, and an awareness of the eternal hope we have through our faith in the risen Christ.

We pray also, O God, for the political leaders of our world. At a time when it is difficult to know whether to wield the sword or to build for security and stability, help leaders to act out of wisdom in defending their people, but also to heed those who call out for peace. We ask for your presence and protection, too, for the many who are being persecuted for their faith. We thank you for their courage and example in being true to their convictions; may their witness be such that those who mistreat them will have their own hearts and souls transformed.

We come to you again with gratitude, O Lord, that you have made us to be people of hope, trusting in your Son Jesus to see us through the most difficult of times, and encouraged by Him to be your reconciling agents in a torn world. May we as a congregation be faithful in our task of proclaiming Him this week, for we ask all of these things in Jesus' Name.

FEBRUARY 14

Valentine's Day

Great and merciful God, Creator of all things, including feelings and emotions, we approach you now with deep reverence, full of gratitude that you love us beyond measure. During this week when we celebrate love on February 14, we acknowledge that yours is the superior love, the unconditional love, the everlasting love. We understand from your Word that love was the motivation for your creation, the covenantal basis for giving us the Ten Commandments, the reason for your mercy and grace. We know from the Gospel and from our own experience that you "so loved the world that you gave us your only begotten Son," Jesus. We appeal to you now, in His Name, for your forgiving love. With sadness we confess our sins, admitting that we often betray your love by breaking the covenant with you, by giving in to temptation, by losing our temper with family members, by being impatient with those we work with, by withholding your love from those who are lonely and desperate. Give us the spiritual strength not only to confess our sins but to turn our lives around in true repentance.

We pray now for the members of our church in the hospital who need your healing love. May they, and all who are suffering, be encouraged by the care of doctors and nurses and the loving support of family and friends. In a moment of silence we pray for others we know who need your mercy and strength, and also for families who need your comfort.

We pray also for those who are most vulnerable to winter cold, construction workers and garbage collectors and those in the service industries; and also for the homeless and the hungry. We thank you for the generosity of your people who have provided warm mittens and necessities of life for the youth on the streets; and for those who on a daily basis work through the food banks and shelters in your loving name.

We pray for those who are motivated by your love to proclaim the Gospel on the mission fields of the world. Give them courage and endurance and safety. May they be encouraged by our prayerful as well as financial support.

We thank you, O Lord, that you trust us with passing on to others the good news of your love. Empower us with your Spirit to have a heart of enthusiasm for doing so, and to demonstrate in practical ways that we are a caring community of faith, for all of this we ask in the Name of Jesus, Our Lord and Saviour and loving Friend.

On this cold and blustery day, help us to appreciate the beauty of the snow rather than be preoccupied with the annoyance of coping with it. Give your Spirit of protection to those travelling on dangerous roads, encouraging them to drive with caution.

Gracious and merciful God, we thank you for your unconditional love – a love that accepts us as we are, and embraces us with warmth and encouragement when we stumble and fall, and a love which forgives us when we rebel against you and hurt others. Help us O God to be faithful in extending that same love to all around us.

Lord of Light, source of all that is eternal – be with us through the dark hours of unease and worry , especially when it seems that the world around us is falling apart because of terrorist attacks and the threat of war. Help us to remember that you are ultimately in charge of all things and that your Spirit of comfort will be with those who have lost loved ones to war and those who are traumatized by conflict. May their faith in you give them hope and the desire to triumph over the evil surrounding them.

O God of mercy and compassion, of comfort and of healing, may the tender touch of your Spirit be upon those in hospital and home who live in illness and fear and despair. Bless them with your peace in the midst of their loneliness and struggle.

On this day called Restorative Justice Sunday, we think of those who are in jail, and of members of their families who feel their own sense of imprisonment; for those who work in the prisons and justice system; and for the victims of crime. May they live in hope through faith in you.

We also bring to you those who suffer ridicule and restriction and violence because of their faith. Give them endurance and courage, we pray, in their distress. Help us not to be indifferent to their struggles; and in fact to identify with them by being courageous in proclaiming our faith in our own community.

We thank you, O God, for the witness of our congregant who is publicly declaring her faith in the risen Christ this morning through the waters of baptism. May her act of devotion be an encouragement to each of us as members of this congregation to be faithful in announcing Jesus as Saviour through the ways in which we speak and act, so that others may have their lives enriched by knowing Him as Lord and Friend. In His name we pray.

Eternal and Almighty God, as we consider the multifaceted universe in which we dwell, as we unite our prayers to you the Creator, as we free our hearts and our minds from worry in your presence, we are filled with awe and wonder. In the serenity of worship, O Lord, your voice becomes clear to us as we reflect on how your Spirit brings fullness of life – how it is good for our souls to hear and respond to your Word and to the music of the ages. Gracious God, we pray that we might truly sense the wonder of who you are and what you have done and are still doing – that we might honour your Holy Name and be united with you and our brothers and sisters in a holy love.

We acknowledge that we need your love, O God, for there are too many ways in which we are not faithful in listening to your voice, or heeding your Word, or showing compassion to one another. We confess that we often think more highly of ourselves than others; that we are selfish and boastful and lustful; and so we ask for your merciful forgiveness in the Name of Christ our Redeemer.

We pray that you would extend your love and peace to those who are in need of healing, O Lord, giving them relief from pain and illness and worry, and an awareness of the prayers and support of family and friends. We thank you for the work of our Parish Nurse and ask you that you would strengthen her as she educates and counsels and facilitates the ministry of healing in body, mind and spirit.

Our hearts are heavy, O Lord, and our eyes are saddened from watching the suffering of many millions in our world affected by bombings and bullets, by poverty and starvation, by disease and grief. May such scenes sober us up in realizing that conflict and discord is the result of prejudice and selfishness and vanity that resides in each of us; so may your Spirit heal us, and inspire us to pattern our lives after Jesus, your Son – to treat other people as He did: where there is suffering, help us bring relief; where there is hatred, love; where there is guilt, forgiveness; where there is fear, courage; where there is hunger, bread.

We thank you, O Lord, for the ways in which you do prompt the members of this congregation to meet the needs of the hungry through the Food Bank and Meals on Wheels and Youth Unlimited and Out of the Cold; the needs of the mentally challenged through the House of Compassion and L'Arche; those in need of housing through Habitat for Humanity; and those in need of spiritual refreshment through Intricity. We ask that all the employees and volunteers will be energized through the realization that they are doing the work of Jesus Himself through their ministry of compassion.

We pray for all who take the Gospel seriously and do what they can to help others to come to know the Saviour. Help each of us to demonstrate our commitment to you by dying to self and coming fully alive to you – that you may use us and our gifts for the spiritual growth of others. Help us to be seeds that bear much fruit, for we ask this and all that we pray for in the name of Jesus, our Saviour and Lord.

ABOUT THE AUTHOR

Deep devotion to Christ and diligent dependability to the members of his congregations marked the ministry of John Torrance to the five Baptist congregations with whom he served in Southern Ontario. During the five years prior to his retirement as Minister of Pastoral Care at Yorkminster Park Baptist Church in Toronto, each Sunday John led the worshipers into the very presence of God with pastoral prayers that reached the hearts of those to whom he ministered. A selection of these prayers makes up this book.

John is a graduate of McMaster University and a past president of the Baptist Convention of Ontario and Quebec. He and his loving wife, Margaret, are blessed with three sons and a granddaughter.

Printed in the United States
133032LV00004B/205-369/P

9 780921 028505